From Great Essays to Research **5**

D0217662

GREAT WRITING

FIFTH EDITION
Keith S. Folse
Tison Pugh

NATIONAL GEOGRAPHIC
L E A R N I N G

Australia · Brazil · Mexico · Singapore · United Kingdom · United States

Great Writing 5: From Great Essays to Research
Keith S. Folse. Tison Pugh

Publisher: Sherrise Roehr

Executive Editor: Laura Le Dréan

Director of Global Marketing: Ian Martin

Product Marketing Manager: Tracy Bailie

Senior Director, Production: Michael Burggren

Production Manager: Daisy Sosa

Content Project Manager: Mark Rzeszutek

Manufacturing Planner: Mary Beth Hennebury

Art Director: Brenda Carmichael

Interior Design: Lisa Trager

Cover Design: Lisa Trager

Composition: SPi-Global

Student Edition: 978-0-357-02086-9
Student Edition with Access Code: 978-0-357-02109-5

National Geographic Learning
20 Channel Center Street
Boston, MA 02210
USA

Cengage learning is a leading provider of customized learning solutions with office locations around the globe, including Singapore, the United Kingdom, Australia, Mexico, Brazil, and Japan. Locate our local office at: **International.cengage.com/region**

Cengage Learning products are represented in Canada by Nelson Education, Ltd.

Visit NGL online at **ELTNGL.com**

Visit our corporate website at **cengage.com**

Printed in China
Print Number: 01   Print Year: 2019

National Geographic photographer Paul Nicklen sits in an inflatable kayak and takes a close-up shot of ice, Skagway, Alaska, USA.

FREEWRITE | Look at the photo and read the caption. On a separate piece of paper, write about what this photograph inspires you to do either personally or professionally.

ELEMENTS OF GREAT WRITING

What Is an Essay?

An **essay** is a written composition on one subject that expresses the views of the writer. In an essay, a writer shares information about a topic with an audience—a teacher, fellow students, or the world beyond the classroom. Most academic essays share a similar structure no matter the topic or length. A well-written essay is organized around three basic parts: an **introduction**, a **body**, and a **conclusion**.

The Five-Paragraph Essay

One of the most commonly taught essays is the five-paragraph essay. This essay has a simple, clear organization, yet it allows writers freedom to explain their ideas on a topic. In a five-paragraph essay, the introduction is paragraph one; the body includes paragraphs two, three, and four; and the conclusion is paragraph five. The essays in this book include **citations**, which are references to outside sources. These sources are listed under **References** at the end of the essay.

Title

Introduction
(Paragraph 1)

Body
(Paragraphs 2–4)

Conclusion
(Paragraph 5)

References

Note that many essays are longer and can have as many body paragraphs as the writer thinks necessary. Writers who understand how to structure a five-paragraph essay with a clear introduction, a detailed body, and a logical conclusion are then ready to add more paragraphs that address increasingly complex and sophisticated ideas.

Kinds of Essays (Rhetorical Modes)

Students often write one kind of essay (called a **rhetorical mode**), such as a cause-effect or comparison essay, at a time. However, in many academic and professional situations, essays are a combination of rhetorical modes. In these essays, paragraphs may serve different purposes and include a mix of rhetorical modes.

Look at two ways to organize an essay titled "Two Plans for the Future of Our City." The first essay compares two plans. The second explains the two plans and shows the effects of each.

ONE RHETORICAL MODE Comparison	MIXED RHETORICAL MODES Definition and focus-on-effects
I. Introduction paragraph Thesis statement: Although the two plans appear to be similar, there are several key differences between Plan A and Plan B.	**I. Introduction paragraph** Thesis statement: In order to choose the best plan for our city, citizens need to fully understand each plan and its potential impact.
II. Body paragraph 1 Compare the objectives of Plan A and Plan B.	**II. Body paragraph 1** Explain Plan A and Plan B in detail.
III. Body paragraph 2 Compare the costs of Plan A and Plan B.	**III. Body paragraph 2** Discuss the effects of Plan A.
IV. Body paragraph 3 Compare the feasibility of Plan A and Plan B.	**IV. Body paragraph 3** Discuss the effects of Plan B.
V. Conclusion paragraph Restate the thesis statement: Plan A and Plan B may initially look similar, but they are in fact quite different.	**V. Conclusion paragraph** Restate the thesis statement: The more that we understand about both of these plans, the better able we are to make the right decision for our future.

Learning how to write an essay using one rhetorical mode increases your ability to construct a mixed-mode essay effectively. In addition, after writing mixed-mode essays, you are better prepared for longer and more complex compositions, such as a research paper.

ACTIVITY 1 | Studying an argument essay

Read Essay 1.1 and answer the questions that follow.

> **WORDS TO KNOW** Essay 1.1
>
> **consistent:** (adj) not changing
> **dispute:** (n) an argument
> **enhance:** (v) to improve
> **for the most part:** (phr) largely, in general
> **innovative:** (adj) using or showing new and creative ideas
>
> **subsequent:** (adj) following
> **tedious:** (adj) tiresome, very boring
> **vastly:** (adv) greatly
> **verify:** (v) to confirm

A man in Egypt votes using a paper ballot.

ESSAY 1.1 **APA**

Against E-Voting

1   Can computer technology be used to steal an election? **For the most part, innovative** technologies promise to make people's lives easier and more comfortable, but these innovations can also be a risk, particularly to democratic processes. Societies should not rely solely on electronic systems for voting because elections are too important to trust to computers.

2   In years past, people voted on paper ballots[1] with a pen. Voters could look over their ballots to ensure that they did not make a mistake. Also, when there was a **dispute** over the results of an election, paper ballots allowed election officials to count votes by hand. This process was **tedious**, but the results could be easily **verified** to see if there were any discrepancies[2] between counts. Several countries still use this traditional system of voting, and it provides a crucial foundation for ensuring fairness.

3   Today, however, voters cannot be sure whether electronic voting systems are reliably counting their votes. For example, a computer hacker[3] could develop a program that redirected a person's vote from one candidate to another. Although some people might think this is unlikely, problems with computer security have occurred throughout the world. The simple fact is that hackers can break into many computer systems for their own purposes. By illegally entering an online polling site, they could change the outcome of an election. Jones and Simons (2012) warn of such a possibility: "a risk of Internet voting is that the computer receiving the voted ballots could be attacked over the Internet by individual hackers, political operatives, foreign governments, or terrorists" (p. 269). Citizens should also question whether electronic voting **enhances** the voting process. As the old saying goes, "If something isn't broken, don't fix it."

[1]ballot: a person's vote as recorded in an election
[2]discrepancy: an unexpected difference
[3]hacker: a person who breaks into a computer network

4   If a government decides to use an electronic voting system, it should ensure that all voters receive receipts for their votes that could then be collected for **subsequent** verification. These receipts would clearly indicate that the vote had gone to the selected candidate. Furthermore, if any candidate suspects that an election is unfair, these receipts could be counted by hand and checked against the computer results. At the very least, as Hale, Montjoy, and Brown (2015) argue, voting should be a simple, secure, and **consistent** process, regardless of the voting procedure being used.

5   Computer technologies have improved the quality of our lives **vastly**, but these technologies are not a cure for all of society's needs. Sometimes a little more human work ensures a better, fairer result. Since voting is critically important to the effective working of society, governments should not rely only on computers for all elections.

References

Hale, K., Montjoy, R., & Brown, M. (2015). *Administering elections*. New York: Palgrave Macmillan. Jones, D., & Simons, B. (2012). *Broken ballots: Will your vote count?* Stanford, CA: CSLI Publications.

1. What is the purpose of this essay? Begin with *The purpose of* . . .

   _____

   _____

2. How many total paragraphs are there? _____ How many body paragraphs? _____

3. **a.** How many citations are used in this essay? _____

   b. What is the list of sources at the end of the essay called? _____

   c. How does the number of citations in the text compare with the number of sources listed at the end of the essay? _____

4. What is the strongest supporting point in the essay? _____

   _____

WRITER'S NOTE Adding Citations

An effective academic essay uses information from outside sources such as academic books, journals, and websites. When using information from outside sources, you must cite where the information comes from. Adding citations within your essay provides information to the reader about these sources. Unit 3 explains how to cite information from sources.

The Introduction Paragraph

An essay begins with an introductory paragraph that tells the reader what to expect to read. A good introduction:

- starts with a **hook** that grabs the reader's attention;
- mentions the **topic** of the essay;
- gives **background information** to connect the reader to the topic;
- and includes a **thesis statement** that gives the main point of the essay and explains the writer's idea or position about the topic.

ACTIVITY 2 | Studying essay introductions

Read the introductory paragraphs in these essays. For each introduction, answer these questions: Does it make you want to read the whole essay? Why or why not?

1. Essay 1.1, "Against E-Voting"

   _____

   _____

2. Essay 1.2, "Camouflage for Survival"

   _____

   _____

3. [Your choice from another unit] Essay _____

   _____

   _____

The Hook

The **hook** is a device used to catch the reader's attention. It is often the opening sentence of an essay. There are a variety of ways to write an effective hook:

TYPE OF HOOK	EXAMPLE
Definition	The dictionary defines gossip as "casual conversation," but gossip is in reality a much more negative interaction.
Quote from a famous person	As entrepreneur Richard Branson said, "There is no planet B. We have to take care of the one we have."
Question	Have you ever thought about where your salad comes from?
Statement that shocks, surprises, or amuses	Each year thousands of teenagers die in driving accidents.
Dilemma/conflict	Some college graduates must decide between an interesting, low-paying job and a more mundane job that pays well.
Comparison (simile or metaphor)	Life is like a roller coaster.

An Arctic fox blends in with the snow while napping.

ACTIVITY 3 | Studying hooks

Read the introduction to each essay and answer the questions. Then discuss with a partner which type of hook is the most effective.

1. Essay 1.1, "Against E-Voting"

   a. Hook: _____

   _____

   b. Which type of hook is it (e.g., definition, quote)? _____

2. Essay 1.2, "Camouflage for Survival"

   a. Hook: _____

   _____

   b. Which type of hook is it? _____

3. Essay 1.3, "Study Skills"

   a. Hook: _____

   _____

   b. What type of hook is it? _____

4. [Your choice from another unit] Essay _____

   a. Hook: _____

   _____

   b. What type of hook is it? _____

> **WRITER'S NOTE** Writing an Effective Hook
>
> Remember, good writers grab their readers' attention with a hook. Look at the two versions of a hook for an essay about a vacation experience.
>
> > It might seem unlikely to catch the flu, lose a wallet, and get a speeding ticket in one afternoon, but these incidents ruined a vacation.
>
> > It was a bad vacation.
>
> The second hook, which uses the verb *be*, is simple and boring. In contrast, the first hook gets the readers' attention by providing details associated with the verbs *catch, lose, get,* and *ruin.* Using specific verbs forces you to provide interesting details that create a better hook.

ACTIVITY 4 | Writing hooks

Read the essay topic, title, and summary. Then write a hook and indicate which type it is. Use a different type of hook for each essay.

1. Topic: Booking a cheap air ticket
    Title: Three Websites for Finding a Cheap Airfare
    Summary: This essay explains the benefits of using three websites to purchase an inexpensive air ticket.

    Hook: _____

    _____

    Type of hook: _____

2. Topic: Remembering all your different passwords
    Title: The Problem of Creating and Remembering Passwords
    Summary: This essay discusses the difficulty that we have remembering all our passwords.

    Hook: _____

    _____

    Type of hook: _____

3. Topic: Choosing the members of a jury
    Title: How Lawyers Select Jury Members
    Summary: This essay considers strategies lawyers use for selecting the members of a jury.

    Hook: _____

    _____

    Type of hook: _____

A farm-to-table chef harvests kale in a vegetable garden.

4. Topic: The benefits of eating kale
Title: An Unexpected Vegetable Ally
Summary: This essay explains four beneficial effects of eating kale daily.

Hook: _____

_____

Type of hook: _____

Thesis Statement and Controlling Idea

An essential part of any essay is the **thesis statement** because it tells a reader what the essay is about and why it was written, its purpose. The thesis statement contains the **controlling idea** of the essay—a word, phrase, or clause that states the writer's opinion or position on the subject. Look at a thesis statement for an essay on the general topic of cell phones in schools:

specific topic   controlling idea
Student use of cell phones in schools should be prohibited.

In this example, the reader expects the essay to give the writer's opinion about why students should not use cell phones in schools.

A good thesis statement often includes the writer's reason or information to support the position. In the example below, the writer gives a reason for his position that societies should not rely only on electronic voting.

controlling idea   specific topic   reason
Societies should not rely solely on electronic systems for voting because elections are too important to trust to computers.

With the topic and controlling idea, a thesis statement provides a blueprint for the organization of the entire essay—it tells the reader what to expect in each body paragraph.

ACTIVITY 5 | Studying examples of thesis statements

Find and write the thesis statement in each essay. Underline the controlling idea. Then write how you expect the information in the essay to be organized.

1. Essay 1.2, "Camouflage for Survival"

   a. Thesis statement: _____

   _____

   b. Expected organization: _____

   _____

2. Essay 1.3, "Study Skills"

   a. Thesis statement: _____

   _____

   b. Expected organization: _____

   _____

3. [Your choice from another unit] Essay _____

   a. Thesis statement: _____

   _____

   b. Expected organization: _____

   _____

ACTIVITY 6 | Comparing thesis statements

Answer these questions about the thesis statements in Activity 5.

1. Which essay's thesis statement most clearly states the controlling idea? Explain your choice.

   _____

   _____

2. Which essay's thesis statement least clearly states the controlling idea? Explain your choice.

   _____

   _____

3. How would you improve one of the thesis statements? Rewrite the thesis statement here.

   _____

   _____

Body Paragraphs

The body of the essay includes two or more **body paragraphs** that explain and support the position and controlling idea in the thesis statement. The body paragraphs develop your thesis statement so that the reader fully comprehends your point of view.

Each body paragraph should include a topic sentence that connects clearly to the controlling idea expressed in the thesis statement. For example, notice how the writer connects the main ideas in each topic sentence back to the thesis statement:

Thesis statement: Societies should not rely only on electronic systems for voting because elections cannot be trusted to computers.

Body Paragraph 1
Topic sentence: Several countries still use a traditional system of voting, and it provides a crucial foundation for ensuring fairness.

Body Paragraph 2
Topic sentence: Today, however, voters cannot be sure whether electronic voting systems are reliably counting their votes.

Body Paragraph 3
Topic sentence: If a government decides to use an electronic voting systems, it should ensure that all voters receive receipts for their votes that could then be collected for subsequent verification.

ACTIVITY 7 | Sequencing body paragraphs

Read the introduction of Essay 1.2. Then put the four body paragraphs in the correct order by numbering them 2 to 5. Underline the topic sentence in each. Do the topic sentences do an effective job of building on the thesis statement? Discuss with a partner.

WORDS TO KNOW Essay 1.2

blend: (v) to fit in
concealing: (adj) hiding
conspicuous: (adj) easily noticeable
distinctive: (adj) clearly distinguishable
evolutionary: (adj) relating to the theory of evolution

flee: (v) to run away; to escape
normal: (adj) usual
predator: (n) an animal that hunts another animal
prey: (n) an animal that is hunted by another animal
vulnerable: (adj) weak

Camouflage for Survival

1   The animals that can live the longest are the ones that hide the best. Animals must protect themselves from **predators** if they are to survive and reproduce, and many accomplish this goal through camouflage. If they hide themselves well, their predators will not see them and thus will not eat them. Camouflage is the end result of many **evolutionary** factors, but it develops primarily as a response to animals' environments. By **blending** in with their surroundings, animals greatly reduce the chance that a predator will locate and kill them. The four primary strategies of camouflage include **concealing** coloration, disruptive coloration, disguise, and mimicry[1].

_____ With mimicry, an animal's coloring makes it resemble another, more dangerous creature so that they are virtually identical. The red, black, and yellow rings of scarlet kingsnakes resemble those of coral snakes. Scarlet kingsnakes are not poisonous, but coral snakes are one of the deadliest species of reptiles. Consequently, the coloring of scarlet kingsnakes scares away their predators, who mistake them for venomous snakes and do not target them for a meal.

_____ Animals such as zebras and giraffes show disruptive coloration. It may seem strange to think that zebras camouflage themselves through their stripes since these features appear quite **distinctive** to humans. The main predators of zebras, however, are lions, and they are colorblind. Thus, a zebra's stripes help the zebra to blend in with the landscapes of grassy plains. Due to their height, giraffes are among the most easily recognized animals on the planet, yet their disruptive coloring allows them to blend in with trees, particularly when they are young and **vulnerable**. Disruptive coloration creates an optical illusion for predators, tricking them about what stands right before their eyes, and so these animals are rarely detected.

[1]mimicry: imitation

Stripes help zebras blend into their environment.

A walking stick insect resting on a leaf in a rain forest

_____ With disguise, some animals resemble specific elements of their surroundings rather than their environment as a whole. The insect known as a walking stick looks very much like a stick, so it is difficult to find it when looking at a tree or bush. Another insect species is referred to as *leaf insects* or *walking leaves* because their bodies so closely look like the plants where they live. Animals camouflage themselves in the seas and oceans as well. The tan coloring and markings of flatfish make them almost impossible to recognize due to the sand around them, despite changes in tides that disturb the ocean's floor.

_____ Concealing coloration helps animals to blend into their surroundings and create a visual illusion. For example, the white coats or feathers of many animals living in arctic zones, such as polar bears and snowy owls, allow them to blend into the background. If a predator looks across a white snow-covered field, it is difficult to pick out its white **prey**. Moreover, some animals can change their colors. Stevens (2016) points out the role of concealment in camouflage: "One likely advantage is that color change enables animals to cope with varying backgrounds and unpredictable environments" (p. 98).

6   None of these strategies of camouflage is more effective than the other, and they all show the range of **normal** possibilities that nature offers animals to survive. Many animals combine camouflage with their "fight or flight" responses, which gives them additional time to decide whether they should stay and fight or **flee**. Furthermore, animals that use camouflage for protection share a **conspicuous** problem as well; as Emlen (2014) observes, "Animals that panic, dashing from their hiding places at the wrong time, or animals that walk or fly with the wrong gait, can break camouflage with deadly consequences" (p. 18). The most effective camouflages keep animals safe from their predators. Whether by concealing coloration, disruptive coloration, disguise, or mimicry, animals need the protections of camouflage if they are to escape their natural foes[2].

[2]foe: an enemy

References

Emlen, D. J. (2014). *Animal weapons: The evolution of battle*. New York: Henry Holt.

Stevens, M. (2016). *Cheats and deceits: How animals and plants exploit and mislead*. Oxford: Oxford University Press.

The Conclusion Paragraph

Well-written essays end with a **conclusion** that restates the thesis. The conclusion should not include any new information. Without a conclusion, an essay seems incomplete and unfinished. A strong conclusion:

- summarizes the writer's main point;
- uses key vocabulary from the introduction paragraph;
- often uses different words to restate the thesis statement;
- may offer a suggestion, give an opinion, make a prediction, or ask a question.

ACTIVITY 8 | Comparing conclusions

Reread the conclusion paragraphs for Essays 1.1 and 1.2 and answer the questions. Then discuss with a partner which conclusion you think is more effective and why.

Essay 1.1, "Against E-Voting"

1. What key words does the writer use from the introduction paragraph?

   _____

2. Paragraph 1 ends with "Societies should not rely solely on electronic systems for voting because elections are too important to trust to computers." How does the conclusion return to this idea?

   _____

   _____

3. Does the writer offer a suggestion, give an opinion, or make a prediction? _____

Essay 1.2, "Camouflage for Survival"

1. What key words does the writer use from the introduction paragraph?

   _____

2. Paragraph 1 ends with "The four primary strategies of camouflage include concealing coloration, disruptive coloration, disguise, and mimicry." How does the conclusion return to this idea?

   _____

   _____

3. Does the writer offer a suggestion, give an opinion, or make a prediction? _____

CONTENTS

CITING SOURCES

Citing Sources in *Great Writing 5*

While the essays in *Great Writing 5* are typically longer than the essays in any of the preceding books in this series, perhaps the most important distinction in the type of writing taught at this level is the use of outside sources.

There are several citation styles that most college or university courses require students to use, but three of the most common are APA (American Psychological Association), MLA (Modern Language Association), and Chicago. These styles include guidelines for writers to help ensure clear and consistent presentation of written information. Guidelines cover areas such as formatting titles and subtitles, indenting paragraphs, numbering pages, and citing sources.

APA is commonly used in the fields of psychology, education, science, and social science. MLA is commonly used in the humanities, including literature, art, and theater. Chicago is commonly used in business, history, and the fine arts. Guidelines for all three methods can be found online or in their respective manual or handbook.

In *Great Writing 5*, we have focused on APA and MLA. Since our students typically take more college courses that require APA, we have given more coverage to this style. However, the main message in of the units is that good writers need to use outside sources and cite those sources following whatever style the instructor has indicated.

Here is how citing sources is presented and practiced in *Great Writing 5*:

Unit 1: Reviewing the Essay	APA
Unit 2: The Writing Process	APA
Unit 3: Using Original Sources	APA and MLA
Unit 4: Cause and Effect	APA
Unit 5: Comparison	MLA
Unit 6: Reaction	APA
Unit 7: Argumentation	MLA
Unit 8: Research Paper	APA

GREAT WRITING MAKES GREAT WRITERS

The new edition of *Great Writing* provides clear explanations, academic writing models, and focused practice to help students write great sentences, paragraphs, and essays. Every unit has expanded vocabulary building, sentence development, and more structured final writing tasks.

1 | Reviewing the Essay

National Geographic photographer Paul Nicklen sits in an inflatable kayak and takes a close-up shot of ice, Skagway, Alaska, USA.

OBJECTIVES
• Review the structure of an essay
• Review the features of introductory, body, and concluding paragraphs
• Write an essay

FREEWRITE Look at the photo and read the caption. On a separate piece of paper, write about what this photograph inspires you to do either personally or professionally.

National Geographic images and content spark students' imaginations and inspire their writing.

Each unit includes:

PART 1: **Elements of Great Writing** teaches the fundamentals of essay and research writing.

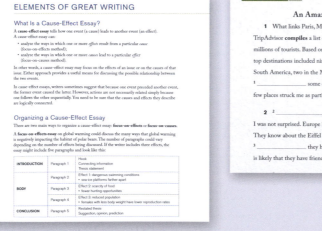

ELEMENTS OF GREAT WRITING

What Is a Cause-Effect Essay?

A **cause-effect essay** tells how one event (a cause) leads to another event (an effect). A cause-effect essay can:

• analyze the ways in which one or more *effects* result from a particular *cause* (focus-on-effects method);
• analyze the ways in which one or more *causes* lead to a particular *effect* (focus-on-causes method).

In other words, a cause-effect essay may focus on the effects of an issue or on the causes of that issue. Either approach provides a useful means for discussing the possible relationship between the two events.

In cause-effect essays, writers sometimes suggest that because one event preceded another event, the former event caused the latter. However, actions are not necessarily related simply because one follows the other sequentially. You need to be sure that the causes and effects they describe are logically connected.

Organizing a Cause-Effect Essay

There are two main ways to organize a cause-effect essay: **focus-on-effects** or **focus-on-causes**.

A **focus-on-effects essay** on global warming could discuss the many ways that global warming is negatively impacting the habitat of polar bears. The number of paragraphs could vary depending on the number of effects being discussed. If the writer includes three effects, the essay might include five paragraphs and look like this:

INTRODUCTION	Paragraph 1	Hook Connecting information Thesis statement
BODY	Paragraph 2	Effect 1: dangerous swimming conditions • sea-ice platforms farther apart
	Paragraph 3	Effect 2: scarcity of food • fewer hunting opportunities
	Paragraph 4	Effect 3: reduced population • females with less body weight have lower reproduction rates
CONCLUSION	Paragraph 5	Restated thesis Suggestion, opinion, prediction

ESSAY 6.2 APA

An Amazing Variety of Travel Destinations

1 What links Paris, Marrakech, and Siam Reap? Each year the travel website TripAdvisor **compiles** a list of the top 25 tourist destinations based on results from millions of tourists. Based on the 2018 **poll** ("Top 25 destinations – World," 2018), the top destinations included nine in Asia, seven in Europe, three in North America, two in South America, two in the Middle East, one in Africa, and one in Australia.
_____ some of the results of this **eagerly** awaited poll were predictable, a few places struck me as particularly interesting choices.

2 ² _____ I saw that seven of the top ten destinations were in Europe, I was not surprised. Europe is popular, and many people dream about going to Europe. They know about the Eiffel Tower in Paris or Buckingham Palace in London ³ _____ they have seen these tourist sites in photos. ⁴ _____, it is likely that they have friends or family who have been there and talked about their trips.

Writing models in both APA and MLA format encourage students to analyze and use the features of great writing in their own work.

Targeted Grammar presents clear explanations and examples that students can immediately apply to their work.

PART 2: Building Better Vocabulary highlights academic words, word associations, collocations, word forms, and vocabulary for writing.

New Words to Know boxes throughout each unit target carefully-leveled words students will frequently use.

PART 3: Building Better Sentences focuses students on sentence-level work to ensure more accurate writing.

PART 4: Writing activities allow students to apply what they have learned by guiding them through the process of writing, editing, and revising.

NEW Test Prep section prepares students for timed writing on high-stakes tests.

SUPPORT FOR INSTRUCTORS AND STUDENTS

FOR INSTRUCTORS

The Classroom Presentation Tool brings the classroom to life by including all Student Book pages, answers, and games to practice vocabulary.

Assessment: ExamView™ allows instructors to create custom tests and quizzes in minutes. **ExamView™** and **Ready to Go Tests** are available online at the teacher companion website for ease of use.

FOR STUDENTS

The Online Workbook provides additional practice in vocabulary, grammar, and writing, plus remediation activities for students who have not mastered at-level vocabulary and grammar.

NEW Guided online writing practice reinforces the writing process, helping students become stronger and more independent writers.

ACKNOWLEDGEMENTS

The Authors and Publisher would like to acknowledge and thank the teachers around the world who participated in the development of the fifth edition of *Great Writing*.

ASIA

Anthony Brian Gallagher, Meijo University, Nagoya

Atsuko Aoki, Aoyama Gakuin University, Tokyo

Atsushi Taguchi, Okayama University of Science, Imabari Campus, Ehime

Helen Hanae, Reitaku University, Kashiwa

Hiroko Shikano, Juchi Medical University, Gotemba

Hisashi Shigematsu, Toyo Gakeun University, Tokyo

Jeremiah L. Hall, Meijo University, Nagoya

Jian Liang Fu, Kwansei Gakuin University, Nishinomiya

Jim Hwang, Yonsei University, Asan

John C. Pulaski, Chuo University and Tokyo Woman's Christian University, Tokyo

Junyawan Suwannarat, Chiang Mai University, Chiang Mai

Katherine Bauer, Clark Memorial International High School, Chiba

Kazuyo Ishibashi, Aoyama Gakuin Univeristy, Tokyo

Lei Na, Jump A-Z, Nanjing

Lor Kiat Seng, Southern University College, Seremban

Mark McClure, Kansai Gaidai University, Osaka

Matthew Shapiro, Konan Boys High School, Ashiya

Nattalak Thirachotikun, Chiang Mai University, Chiang Rai

Nick Boyes, Meijo University, Nagoya

Nick Collier, Ritsumeikan Uji Junior and Senior High School, Kobe

Olesya Shatunova, Kanagawa University, Yokohama

Pattanapichet Fasawang, Bangkok University International College, Bangkok

Paul Hansen, Hokkaido University, Sapporo

Paul Salisbury, Aichi University, Nagoya

Randall Cotten, Gifu City Women's College, Gifu

Sayaka Karlin, Toyo Gakuen University, Tokyo

Scott Gray, Clark Memorial International High School Umeda Campus, Osaka

Selina Richards, HELP University, Kuala Lumpur

Terrelle Bernard Griffin, No. 2 High School of East China Normal University-International Division, Shanghai

William Pellowe, Kinki University, Fukuoka

Yoko Hirase, Hiroshima Kokusai Gakuin University, Hiroshima

Youngmi Lim, Shinshu University, Matsumoto

Zachary Fish, RDFZ Xishan School AP Center, Beijing

USA

Amanda Kmetz, BIR Training Center, Chicago, Illinois

Amy Friedman, The American Language Institute, San Diego, California

Amy Litman, College of Southern Nevada, Las Vegas, Nevada

Angela Lehman, Virginia Commonwealth University, Richmond, Virginia

Aylin Bunk, Mount Hood Community College, Portland, Oregon

Barbara Silas, South Seattle College, Seattle, Washington

Bette Brickman, College of Southern Nevada, Las Vegas, Nevada

Breana Bayraktar, Northern Virginia Community College, Fairfax, Virginia

Carolyn Ho, Lone Star College-CyFair, Cypress, Texas

Celeste Flowers, University of Central Arkansas, Conway, Arkansas

Christina Abella, The College of Chicago, Chicago, Illinois

Christine Lines, College of Southern Nevada, Las Vegas, Nevada

Clare Roh, Howard Community College, Columbia, Maryland

DeLynn MacQueen, Columbus State Community College, Columbus, Ohio

Eleanor Molina, Northern Essex Community College, Lawrence, Massachusetts

Emily Brown, Hillsborough Community College, Florida

Emily Cakounes, North Shore Community College, Medford, Massachusetts

Erica Lederman, BIR Training Center, Chicago, Illinois

Erin Zoranski, Delaware Technical Community College, Wilmington, Delaware

Eugene Polissky, University of Potomac, Washington, DC

Farideh Hezaveh, Northern Virginia Community College, Sterling, Virginia

Gretchen Hack, Community College of Denver, Denver, Colorado

Heather Snavely, California Baptist University, Riverside, California

Hilda Tamen, University of Texas Rio Grande Valley, Edinburg, Texas

Holly Milkowart, Johnson County Community College, Overland Park, Kansas

Jessica Weimer, Cascadia College, Bothell, Washington

Jill Pagels, Lonestar Community College, Houston, Texas

Jonathan Murphy, Virginia Commonwealth University, Richmond, Virginia

Joseph Starr, Houston Community College, Southwest, Houston, Texas

Judy Chmielecki, Northern Essex Community College, Lawrence, Massachusetts

Kate Baldridge-Hale, Valencia College, Orlando, Florida

Kathleen Biache, Miami Dade College, Miami, Florida

Katie Edwards, Howard Community College, Columbia, Maryland

Kenneth Umland, College of Southern Nevada, Las Vegas, Nevada

FROM THE AUTHORS

Great Writing began in 1998 when three of us were teaching writing and frequently found ourselves complaining about the lack of materials for English language learners. A lot of books talked about writing but did not ask the students to write until the end of a chapter. In essence, the material seemed to be more of a lecture followed by "Now you write an essay." Students were reading a lot but writing little. What was missing was useful sequenced instruction for developing ESL writers by getting them to write.

Each of us had folders with our own original tried-and-true activities, so we set out to combine our materials into a coherent book that would help teachers and students alike. The result was *Great Paragraphs* and *Great Essays*, the original books of the *Great Writing* series. Much to our surprise, the books were very successful. Teachers around the world reached out to us and offered encouragement and ideas. Through the past four editions we have listened to those ideas, improved upon the books, and added four more levels.

We are proud to present this 5th edition of the *Great Writing* series with the same tried-and-true focus on writing and grammar, but with an added emphasis on developing accurate sentences and expanding level-appropriate academic vocabulary.

We thank those who have been involved in the development of this series over the years. In particular for the 5th edition, we would like to thank Laura Le Dréan, Executive Editor; the developmental editors for this edition: Lisl Bove, Eve Einselen Yu, Yeny Kim, Jennifer Monaghan, and Tom Jefferies. We will be forever grateful to two people who shaped our original books: Susan Maguire and Kathy Sands-Boehmer. Without all of these professionals, our books would most definitely not be the great works they are right now.

As always, we look forward to hearing your feedback and ideas as you use these materials with your students.

Sincerely,

Keith Folse
April Muchmore-Vokoun
Elena Vestri
David Clabeaux
Tison Pugh

1 | Reviewing the Essay

OBJECTIVES
- Review the structure of an essay
- Review the features of introductory, body, and concluding paragraphs
- Write an essay

ACTIVITY 9 | Writing a conclusion paragraph

Read Essay 1.3. Then, on a separate piece of paper, write a conclusion paragraph. Use the introduction, the thesis statement, and the topic sentences of the body paragraphs to help you.

WORDS TO KNOW Essay 1.3

acronym: (n) a word constructed from the initials of other words (e.g., *FIFA*)
advocate: (v) to endorse
coherent: (adj) rational, logically connected
cram: (v) to stuff; to shove into

dread: (v) to fear
endure: (v) to suffer through an experience
pace: (v) to undertake a task at a steady rate
retain: (v) to keep; to hold

ESSAY 1.3   **APA**

Study Skills

1   Many students **dread** them, but tests are a key part of the educational experience. To be prepared for the various exams they must **endure** over the years of their education, students should develop study skills that help them learn a range of new academic materials with maximum comprehension. A wide variety of study skills and techniques can aid students as they work towards their objectives in all of their classes.

2   One of the most important and simplest ways to prepare for exams is to attend all classes and to take notes on lectures and discussions. For effective studying, however, these notes must be meaningful and **coherent**, as Ritchie and Thomas (2015) point out: "notes will mean nothing when you return to them unless you have understood the material in the first place and incorporated this understanding into your notes" (p. 36). Students should not write down everything they hear but instead, write down key words and phrases that will remind them of the issues that were discussed. By focusing on the most important topics of the lecture or discussion in their note-taking, students will improve their understanding of the lesson. After class, students should review their notes to clarify their meaning and to determine what information is supplementary, but not essential, to the lessons.

3   Studying for an exam requires memorizing large amounts of information. Study techniques such as mnemonic[1] devices and flash cards can help students accomplish this task. In one common mnemonic device, the exact colors of what we see as white light are associated with the corresponding made-up name "ROY G. BIV," an **acronym** that stands for *red, orange, yellow, green, blue, indigo,* and *violet.* Flash cards also help students to develop their memory and to learn new information. The use of flash cards is an appropriate memorization technique when a student is learning a lot of new information, such as vocabulary words of a new language or scientific terms for a biology class. Students can also rearrange the cards to ensure that they are learning each term separately and not simply memorizing the order of the cards.

[1]mnemonic: related to memory

4   While memorization is an important part of studying, students should also seek to enhance their understanding of the main concepts in their courses. To this end, Reynolds (2002) **advocates** the SQ3R (Survey, Question, Read, Recite, Review) method to help students understand the subject matter throughout their reading and study (pp. 152–155). Before each assignment, students should look over the material to get a general sense of the information they are expected to learn and its overall context. Next, students formulate questions about this material, trying to anticipate what they will be expected to learn. Students then read the assignment, looking for the answers to the questions they created in the previous step. For the fourth step, students recite or restate what they learned. Finally, students must frequently review the materials. Reynolds cautions students that "most forgetting takes place within twenty-four hours," and so they must "review the reading selection to **retain**" the information (p. 155).

5   Time management skills are another necessary component of effective studying. Many students simply "**cram** for the exam," but this strategy limits long-term learning because students then forget information they have put in their short-term memory. Bedford and Wilson (2013) advise students to **pace** themselves throughout the course of the semester and "to work at times when you can perform at your best for your study time. . . . It is not sensible to work until you are exhausted and cannot concentrate" (p. 142). Thus, the single most effective strategy for studying is to see it as a long process stretching over the semester rather than as a rushed session the night before each test.

References

Bedford, D., & Wilson, E. (2013). *Study skills for Foundation degrees* (2nd ed). London: Routledge.

Reynolds, J. (2002). *Succeeding in college: Study skills and strategies* (2nd ed). Upper Saddle River, NJ: Prentice Hall.

Ritchie, C., & Thomas, P. (2015). *Successful study* (2nd ed). London: Routledge.

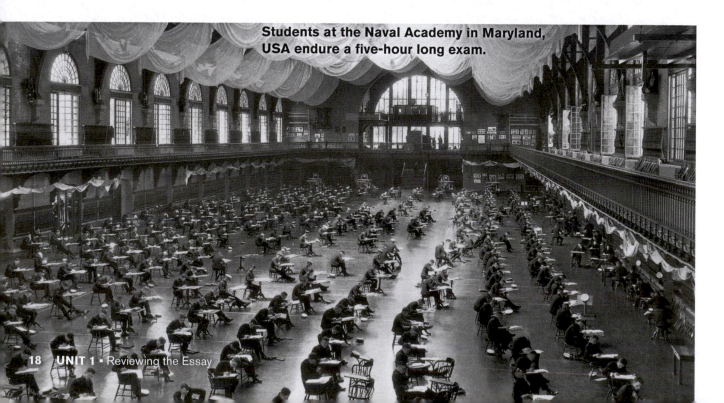

Students at the Naval Academy in Maryland, USA endure a five-hour long exam.

Grammar: Modifying Nouns

Nouns can be modified in several ways.

NOUN MODIFIERS	EXAMPLES
A preceding adjective	The **main** <u>reason</u> for this situation is complex. TripAdvisor is a **well-known** and **reputable** <u>organization</u>.
A prepositional phrase	A lack of money is the <u>reason</u> **for this decision.** Inflation is one of the <u>problems</u> **with the economy.**
An adjective clause	This is the <u>reason</u> **that the committee voted no.** These are <u>problems</u> **that are happening now.**
A noun + noun phrase	In 2018, the United Nations produced a **science** <u>report</u>. Learn this **target** <u>word</u>.

Note that a noun + noun phrase can have several nouns acting as adjectives:

a **research** paper   a **history research** paper

A noun + noun phrase can also include an adjective; it precedes a noun acting as an adjective:

a **long** research paper   a **long** history research paper

ACTIVITY 10 | Understanding nouns modifying adjectives

Write a short definition of these items.

1. a weather delay _____

2. a money shortage _____

3. a rice cooker _____

4. an air traffic control mistake _____

5. an earthquake warning system malfunction _____

ACTIVITY 11 | Identifying noun + noun phrases

Underline the six noun + noun phrases in the paragraph.

If government officials decide to use electronic voting machines, they should ensure that all voters show proper voter registration before voting and then receive paper receipts after voting. These receipts could then be collected for later verification. These paper slips would clearly state that the voters really voted for the candidates that they selected. Furthermore, if any candidate suspects that an election is unfair, these receipts could be counted by hand and checked against the official results that the computers provided. At the very least, voting should be a simple, secure, and consistent process, regardless of the voting procedure that is being used.

BUILDING BETTER VOCABULARY

WORDS TO KNOW

acronym (n)	distinctive (adj) AW	pace (v)
advocate (v) AW	dread (v)	predator (n) AW
blend (v)	endure (v)	prey (n) AW
coherent (adj) AW	enhance (v) AW	retain (v) AW
concealing (adj)	evolutionary (adj) AW	subsequent (adj) AW
consistent (adj) AW	flee (v)	tedious (adj)
conspicuous (adj)	for the most part (phr)	vastly (adv)
cram (v)	innovative (adj) AW	verify (v)
dispute (n)	normal (adj) AW	vulnerable (adj)

ACTIVITY 12 | Word associations

Circle the word that is most closely related to the word on the left.

1. acronym	east	UFO
2. conceal	find	hide
3. dispute	disagreement	disappearance
4. enhance	decrease	increase
5. normal	special	usual
6. pace	speed	weight
7. predator	attacker	worrier
8. retain	exit	keep
9. vastly	quickly	significantly
10. verify	check	locate

ACTIVITY 13 | Collocations

Fill in the blank with the word that most naturally completes the phrase.

blend	flee	risk	subsequent	vastly

1. in _____ months

2. _____ from the scene

3. _____ into your surroundings

4. take an unnecessary _____

5. a _____ different result

coherent	dread	enhance	normal	endure

6. _____ seeing the dentist

7. _____ hardships

8. a(n) _____ strategy

9. a(n) _____ body temperature

10. _____ the flavor

ACTIVITY 14 | Word forms

Complete each sentence with the correct word form. Use the correct form of the verbs.

NOUN	VERB	ADJECTIVE	ADVERB	SENTENCES
deviation	deviate	deviant		**1.** A strict project manager does not allow any _____ from the schedule. **2.** If an essay _____ from the assignment, it will not receive a good grade.
endurance	endure	enduring		**3.** Marathon runners need to have a lot of physical _____. **4.** Last summer, residents of Los Angeles _____ several days of extreme heat.
enhancement	enhance	enhanced		**5.** Compared to the old version, the new laptop has _____ features. **6.** Arriving early _____ your chances of getting a good seat at a concert.
evolution	evolve	evolved		**7.** The English language _____ considerably over time. Middle English sounds quite different to us today. **8.** Intelligent life was slow to _____ on Earth.
vastness		vast	vastly	**9.** The Chinese and Vietnamese languages are _____ different. **10.** In Canada, there are _____ areas of land with few people.

A three-banded armadillo can curl into a ball inside its bony shell for protection from predators.

ACTIVITY 15 | Vocabulary in writing

Choose five words from Words to Know. Write a complete sentence with each word.

1. _____

2. _____

3. _____

4. _____

5. _____

BUILDING BETTER SENTENCES

ACTIVITY 16 | Editing

Each sentence has two errors. Find and correct them.

1. The candidates TV commercial was crucial part of her campaign.

2. Some animals have develop very clever ways of protect themselves.

3. In many course, the final exam is worth as much as 50% of final grade.

4. The three largest countries in the South America is Brazil, Argentina, and Colombia.

5. Sell a product successfully in a foreign country may require to make changes to the product.

Combining Sentences

Some writers use short sentences because they feel that they will make mistakes if they write longer, more complicated sentences. However, longer sentences that connect ideas together are often easier for readers to understand.

Study these three sentences. The important information is circled.

The (Treaty of Paris) was (signed) in (1783.)

The Treaty of Paris (ended the American Revolution.)

The Treaty of Paris (established the United States.)

The most important information from each sentence can be used to create longer, more coherent sentences. The sentences below are good ways to combine the shorter sentences:

When the Treaty of Paris was signed in 1783, it ended the American Revolution and established the United States.

In 1783, the Treaty of Paris ended the American Revolution and established the United States.

ACTIVITY 17 | Combining sentences

Combine the ideas into one sentence. You may change the word forms, but do not change or omit any ideas. There may be more than one answer.

1. The main cause of the problem is a lack of natural resources.
    These natural resources include coal and oil.
    This lack of resources is severe.

    _____

    _____

2. The president played a part in passing a bill.
    The vice-president played a part in passing a bill.
    The bill raises taxes on sodas.
    The bill raises taxes on other sugary drinks.

    _____

    _____

3. In the experiment, the scientists placed coffee plants in special containers.
    The purpose of the experiment was to see how much oxygen the plants would produce.
    The experiment was last week.

    _____

    _____

ACTIVITY 18 | Responding to teacher feedback

Read the teacher's comments. Then rewrite the paragraph on a separate piece of paper.

PARAGRAPH 1.1

No Babies Allowed?

interesting topic and good hook

"this" what?

always true?

word choice

too strong

word choice

combine sentences

add verb

missing article

add transition

      Should parents be allowed to bring their young baby to an upscale restaurant? Recently there has been some debate about this. Restaurant customers complain that a crying baby can ruin their special evening out. They say that it is not OK that they have paid a lot of money for a special evening and then a crying baby spoils their experience. Parents say that everyone has the right to eat in any restaurant. For them, the price of the meal should not determine who can and cannot eat at that restaurant. Restaurant owners find themselves in a bad situation. They do not want to lose affluent customers who willing to spend a lot of money at their places of business. However, these same owners do not want to appear to be cold-hearted when it comes to children. It is indeed difficult situation. It appears that different restaurants will have different policies about customers bringing young babies with them.

A family eats Sunday breakfast at a child-friendly restaurant in Hong Kong.

WRITING

In the next unit you will review the steps in the writing process and then, in later units, use those steps to practice writing different kinds of essays. In this section, you will think about what you already know about four of the rhetorical modes.

ACTIVITY 19 | Matching topics to rhetorical modes

Look at the writing topics below. Match the topic (1–4) with the kind of essay you think you would write.

TOPIC 1: Which of two local tourist attractions is more popular?

TOPIC 2: Write about a great movie you have seen.

TOPIC 3: Agree or disagree with this statement: We use cell phones too much.

TOPIC 4: What happens when people do not get enough sleep?

1. A cause-effect essay: _____

2. A comparison essay: _____

3. A reaction essay: _____

4. An argumentative essay: _____

ACTIVITY 20 | Writing an essay

Write an essay on one of the topics in Activity 19. Use at least two of the vocabulary words or phrases from the Words to Know list. Underline them in your essay.

TEST PREP

Write an essay of three to five paragraphs about the following topic. You should spend about 40 minutes on this task.

If you could meet one famous person, living or dead, who would it be? Explain why you would choose to meet this person and what you would hope to gain from the experience.

Begin your essay with an effective hook and a good thesis statement. Finish with a suggestion, an opinion, or a prediction.

> **TIP**
>
> Before beginning to write, read the writing prompt several times to make sure you understand it. Circle key words or phrases that tell you what type of writing you should be doing (e.g., "Explain," "Give your opinion," "Compare"). Then underline key content words. Focusing on these words will help you brainstorm ideas.

2 | The Writing Process

A woman and her son in Nam Dinh, Vietnam, follow the traditional process of bundling decoratively dyed incense and laying it out to dry.

FREEWRITE | Look at the photo and read the caption. On a separate piece of paper, write about a process you know well.

ELEMENTS OF GREAT WRITING

What Is the Writing Process?

A good essay results from effective planning. You must plan your ideas before writing the first word of the first sentence of the first paragraph. Many students make the mistake of trying to start writing without proper planning. In fact, before writing the first word of your essay, you should have already planned the introduction paragraph, the general ideas of each of the body paragraphs, and the message of the conclusion. Of course, many of these ideas will be modified throughout the writing process, but a good essay begins with planning, not writing.

You can use the following steps to move from the initial idea for your essay to the final draft. It is important to keep in mind that writing an essay is not a linear process, and you may go back and forth between these steps multiple times.

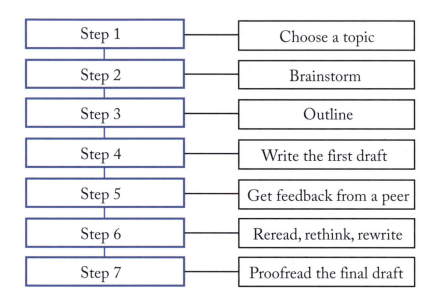

Step 1	Choose a topic
Step 2	Brainstorm
Step 3	Outline
Step 4	Write the first draft
Step 5	Get feedback from a peer
Step 6	Reread, rethink, rewrite
Step 7	Proofread the final draft

ACTIVITY 1 | Your writing process

Imagine your teacher has given you the following assignment:

Cell phones have changed our lives. Write an essay that discusses two or three positive or negative effects of cell phones. The essay should be between 800 and 1,200 words long.

What are three things you should do before you write the essay?

1. _____

2. _____

3. _____

Steps in Writing an Essay

Step 1: Choose a Topic

Every essay addresses a specific topic. The choice of the topic is important because topics should not be too general. For example, "technology" is too large a topic to be covered in one essay. Likewise, topics should not be too specific, such as "how to turn on a cell phone" because it would be difficult to write more than one paragraph about it.

Sometimes an instructor may assign a topic, but other times you may need to think of one yourself. For some writing assignments, you must choose a topic from a list of suggestions. For example, an instructor might ask students to write about one of the following topics:

- Write a cause-effect essay illustrating the effects of technology on people's lives.

- Compare the characteristics of two fast-food restaurants.

- Discuss the three most important qualities of a good friend.

As you consider possible topics, ask yourself these questions:

1. What do I know about this topic?
2. What do my readers know?
3. What else do I need to know?
4. Do I need to research this topic?
5. What is the task asking me to do? Explain a cause? Explain an effect? Compare? Contrast? Describe? Persuade?

Answering these questions will help you select the best topic for your assignment and develop ideas about that topic into an essay.

ACTIVITY 2 | Choosing a topic

Choose one of the topics from Step 1 for an essay. Write at least two reasons why you chose it. Consider the five questions above.

_____

_____

_____

_____

_____

ACTIVITY 3 | Narrowing topics

Read the four general topics and the corresponding specific topic for each. Then write two more specific topics for each general topic that could be addressed in an essay.

GENERAL TOPICS	SPECIFIC TOPIC
1. Music and behavior	a. How music affects shopping habits
	b.
	c.
2. Jobs in the 21st century	a. Opportunities in the new "gig" economy
	b.
	c.
3. Sports and culture	a. The rising popularity of extreme sports
	b.
	c.
4. Health and nutrition	a. A comparison of three diet programs
	b.
	c.

A rock climber ascends to extreme heights in Yosemite National Park, California.

Step 2: Brainstorm

The next step in writing an essay is to generate ideas about the topic by brainstorming. There are several good ways to organize your ideas as you brainstorm—using a mind map, completing a Venn diagram, or drawing a T-chart. Here is an example of a mind map for the topic: "Write a cause-effect essay illustrating the effects of technology on people's lives."

The general topic is "technology and people." Because the assignment is a cause-effect essay, the writer must explain some of the effects that the cause (*technology*) has on our lives. Notice how the writer brainstormed three specific topics with ideas for each.

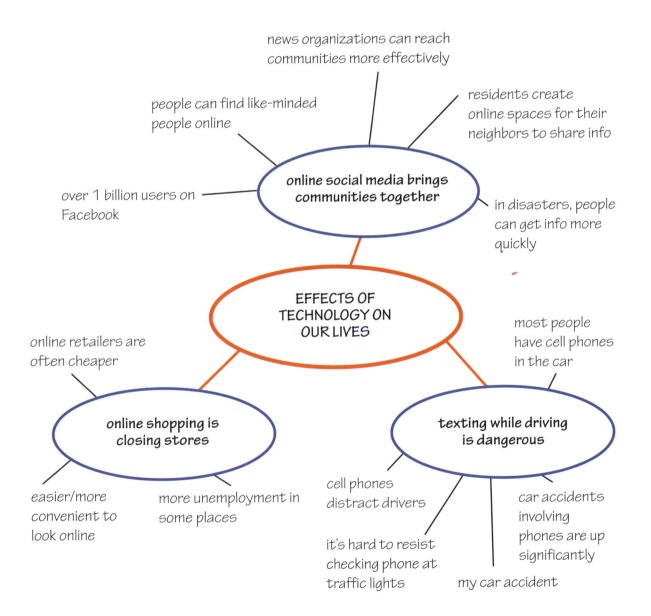

When you have brainstormed several ideas, you should select the ones that you can use to write a well-developed essay. At this point, you should think about the thesis statement for your essay. There should be a clear relationship between the ideas that you choose in this brainstorming step and your final thesis statement.

ACTIVITY 4 | Brainstorming a topic

Use the T-chart to brainstorm ideas about the topic "Limiting children's screen time." Compare your notes with a partner's.

PROS	CONS
interact more with people	hard to inform time limit

Step 3: Outline

After brainstorming ideas, the next step is to make an outline. An outline helps you to organize the information and support the thesis. It also helps you to see which areas of the essay are strong and which are weak.

Formal outlines use Roman numerals (I, II, III, . . .) and capital letters (A, B, C, . . .) to show different levels of information. Some outlines consist of only short phrases; others include complete sentences. Use the type of outline that will help you write a great essay.

While the introduction paragraph must come first and the conclusion last, the body paragraphs can be structured in a variety of ways. When organizing an outline, you should determine the logical sequence of your ideas and how you will move from one paragraph to another. Keep in mind that there is no single correct way to organize an essay.

Here is an example outline for the topic "Write a cause-effect essay illustrating the effects of technology on people's lives." Notice how the writer used short phrases and sentences.

Title: *Some Positive Effects of Computers on Society*

I. Introduction

    A. Hook

    B. Background information

    C. Thesis statement: *Some people say that computers have harmed people's lives, but computers have helped society in two significant areas: information and education.*

II. Topic of Body Paragraph 1: *Effects on information*

    A. Effect 1

    B. Effect 2

III. Topic of Body Paragraph 2: *Effects on education*

    A. Effect 1

    B. Effect 2

IV. Conclusion

    A. Restated thesis

    B. Prediction: *In time, these two areas will continue to improve in ways we can only begin to imagine now.*

ACTIVITY 5 | Outlining a topic

On a separate piece of paper, write an outline for the topic you brainstormed in Activity 4.

ACTIVITY 6 | Understanding the organization of an essay

Complete this draft outline of Essay 2.1, "The Dangers of Texting While Driving," with information listed below (a–h).

a. Police officer gave me a ticket.
b. People think using a cell phone does not affect ability to do other things at same time.
c. I was expecting a text message.
d. Advice—turn your cell phone off.
e. My car accident was completely avoidable—I was texting while driving.
f. I took my eyes off the road.
g. Texting causes the same delayed reaction as driving while drinking.
h. Cell phones are addictive.

Title: The Dangers of Texting While Driving

I. Introduction

    A. Hook: Establish that texting while driving is dangerous.

    B. Thesis statement: _a_

II. Topic of Body Paragraph 1: Beginning of the story

    A. _h_

    B. I answered the message.

    C. _f_

III. Topic of Body Paragraph 2: My accident could have been worse.

    A. I had an accident. I hit a parking meter.

    B. _e_

IV. Topic of Body Paragraph 3: People feel a strong need to answer their cell phones.

    A. _____

    B. Answering a text while driving is not rational.

V. Topic of Body Paragraph 4: _b_

    A. The Occupational Safety and Health administration warns drivers that reaction time is greatly slowed down.

    B. Example: _g_

VI. Conclusion

    A. The ending of the story is not as bad as it could have been.

    B. _d_

Step 4: Write the First Draft

The most important thing in writing a first draft is to write it. Too many writers spend hours trying to write a perfect first draft. A much better strategy is to draft ideas on paper and then edit your words to match what you really intend to say. If you are having a hard time with one sentence, just make a note like "Add sentence about this idea later" and then keep writing.

WRITER'S NOTE Pausing after the First Draft

After writing a first draft, one of the most effective strategies is to set your essay aside for a few hours or even a few days. When reading your paper again, you may find several places where you want to change words or add ideas. In this case, the time between when you wrote the paper and when you reread helps you see it from a different perspective.

Step 5: Get Feedback from a Peer

A good way to generate ideas about improving your writing is to ask someone to look at your ideas and organization. Peer editing is commonly used for first drafts, but it can also be useful for hooks and outlines and in every step in the writing process.

When editing someone else's work, be helpful. If something is not clear, write something like "This sentence is not clear" or "Can you think of an example to support this idea?"

The peer editing forms for your essays and research paper in Units 2–8 (see the *Writer's Handbook*) will help you to focus on specific areas to examine in each piece. Here are a few general points that a peer editor considers:

- Does every sentence have a subject and a verb and express a complete thought?
- Are there any sentences or sections that do not make sense?
- Even if I do not agree with the writer's viewpoint, do I understand the writer's line of thinking?

Peer editing a draft is a critical step toward the final goal of a polished essay. Your essay will be greatly helped by the fresh perspective a new reader can give. It is often difficult, even for highly skilled writers, to see the weaknesses of their own writing. Remember that professional writers have editors, so do not be embarrassed to ask for help.

ACTIVITY 7 | Using a peer editing form

Study the example peer editing form on the next page. Read each question and decide if it would be easy or difficult for you to answer if you were reading another writer's paper. Then choose an essay from Unit 1 and complete the peer editing form.

Sample Peer Editing Form

Reader: _____   **Date:** _____

1. What is the general topic of the essay? _____

2. How many paragraphs are there? _____

3. Does the introduction do a good job of introducing the topic?   ❑ Yes ❑ No

If not, what suggestions can you offer for improving it?

_____

_____

4. Can you identify the thesis statement?   ❑ Yes ❑ No

If so, write it here.

_____

5. Do you agree with the writer's ideas about this topic? Why or why not? Explain your answer and give examples of things you agree or disagree with.

_____

_____

6. Does the conclusion follow logically from the body of the essay?   ❑ Yes ❑ No

If not, what suggestions can you offer?

_____

_____

Step 6: Reread, Rethink, Rewrite

Once you have received comments from a peer, use that feedback to improve the essay in the second draft. You have at least four choices in responding to the feedback:

1. **Do nothing.** If you think the peer editor's comments are not correct or not helpful, then do nothing. However, remember that if one reader had a problem with your essay, perhaps other readers will encounter the same problem.

2. **Add information.** If the reader found any unclear ideas or needed any parts clarified, then you might want to add more information. For example, you might need to add identifying information, so instead of writing "The solution is actually quite easy," you could write "The solution to the problem of Internet security is actually quite easy."

3. **Cut information.** If the reader thinks that your writing is wordy or that a certain sentence is not related to the topic, then you should remove the wordiness or omit the sentence.

4. **Improve vocabulary.** Change vocabulary if the reader thinks the word choices are not academic enough, are unclear, or are too vague.

ACTIVITY 8 | Responding to feedback

Read the teacher's comments on a student's first draft of a paragraph. Then rewrite the paragraph on a separate piece of paper.

> **WORDS TO KNOW** Paragraph 2.1
>
> **bargain:** (v) to come to an agreement
> **desire:** (n) a want, wish
> **maximize:** (v) to increase to the highest amount
>
> **negotiable:** (adj) open to discussion
> **strategize:** (v) to make a plan
> **tough:** (adj) difficult

PARAGRAPH 2.1

The Value of Bargaining

too vague

Bargaining for the best price when you are shopping is a **tough** thing. The buyer

wrong word   *combine*

wants to take a product at the lowest possible price. The seller wants to **maximize** the

not academic

potential for profit. While the **desires** of the buyer and the seller really oppose each other,

who?

it is in the best interest of these people to **strategize** exactly how they will convince a seller

always true?

to lower his/her prices. Although prices are not **negotiable**, it never hurts to bargain with

the seller.

At the Merkato in Addis Ababa, Ethiopia, the largest open-air market in Africa, bargaining is art and entertainment.

ACTIVITY 9 | Cutting unnecessary information

Read Essay 2.1 and underline one sentence or question in each paragraph that is not necessary or does not contain important information.

WORDS TO KNOW Essay 2.1

anticipate: (v) to expect something to happen
at once: (adv) immediately
demonstrate: (v) to explain, show
harm: (n) injury, hurt
interchangeable: (adj) capable of being used in the place of another thing
minor: (adj) not serious
multitask: (v) to do several activities at the same time

occupational: (adj) relating to a job
rational: (adj) logical, intelligent
shift: (v) to change
thereby: (adv) as a result
tragic: (adj) causing extreme distress or sadness
up to: (adv) to the point of, to the extent of
virtually: (adv) for the most part

ESSAY 2.1 | **APA**

The Dangers of Texting While Driving

1 Texting while driving is dangerous, but many people continue to do so. Fortunately, my own experiences with texting and driving did not result in a horrible accident, and the damage to my car was relatively **minor**. While I did not suffer bodily injury, the damage to my ego was severe. My car accident was completely avoidable because I was texting while driving. The vehicle I was driving at the time was approximately five years old.

2 I have always thought of myself as a good driver. I pay attention to the road, **anticipate** the actions of other drivers, and am very aware of how road conditions can **shift** instantly. One day when I was driving to my job on roads I have traveled countless times, my cell phone beeped to indicate that I had a new text message. Every day I receive **up to** 50 text messages. I knew a friend would text me that morning to let me know about his plans for the evening, and I also knew that I should write back quickly to tell him that I could not join him. Unfortunately, that is when I took my eyes off the road, **thereby** setting the stage for the accident.

3 My accident could have had a much worse ending. Thankfully, I was not on a major highway, but rather on a quiet street early in the morning. The only result of my accident was that I drove onto a sidewalk and hit a parking meter. The police gave me a ticket for the damage I had done. The police who arrived at the accident scene were very polite.

4 Psychologists have **demonstrated** that texting is addictive (Gutiérrez, de Fonseca, and Rubio, 2016). When phones make that sweet sound of new texts arriving, people want to read those messages **at once**. According to Hayley Tsukayama's article (2018), the World Health Organization says that video games are a serious addiction for millions of people. We like to believe that we usually make **rational** decisions, but reading a text while driving is not a rational choice at all.

5 Drivers think they can successfully **multitask**, but they are wrong. No matter how good drivers might be, they must eliminate all distractions, including cell phones. Some cell phones can help drivers immediately call for emergency help if an accident occurs. The **Occupational Safety and Health Administration (2012)**, a division of the United States Department of Labor, warns drivers: "Reaction time is delayed for a driver talking on a cell phone as much as it is for a driver who is legally drunk." Many people who understand the danger of drinking and driving do not think they will cause any **harm** if they text and drive, but they must learn that the two activities are **virtually interchangeable** in terms of the dangers they create on the road.

6 Why do people continue to mix texting and driving? Other than the cost of a ticket and a parking meter, my story has a happy ending. Many other people, both drivers and innocent pedestrians[1], are not so lucky, as documented by the **tragic** stories on social media. Learn from my experience and those detailed online—and turn your cell phone off so that you will arrive safely at your next destination.

[1]pedestrians: people walking

References

Gutiérrez, J., de Fonseca, F., & Rubio, G. (2016). "Cell-phone addiction: A review." *Frontiers in psychiatry,* 7. Retrieved from https://doi.org/10.3389/fpsyt.2016.00175

Occupational Safety and Health Administration. (2016). Distracted driving: No texting [Brochure]. Retrieved from https://www.osha.gov/

Tsukayama, H. (2018 June 18). Video game addiction is a real condition, WHO says. Here's what that means. *Washington Post.* Retrieved from https://www.washingtonpost.com/news/the-switch/wp/2018/06/18/video-game-addiction-is-a-real-condition-who-says-heres-what-that-means/

Step 7: Proofread the Final Draft

Proofreading gives you the opportunity to correct grammar and spelling errors. Careless mistakes make your writing look sloppy and get in the way of clear communication. Proofreading is not just about grammar and spelling errors, however. Even at this late stage, you can add or change words, or even sentences and paragraphs, to make your essay better. It is essential to proofread your final essay carefully before turning it in to your teacher.

Again, if it is possible to wait a few days between your editing stage and the final proofreading, you will be able to see your paper more objectively.

WRITER'S NOTE Adding a Title

One of the fastest ways to get a reader interested in your essay is through the use of an interesting title. A good title can also help readers better guess the content of your essay. Using an idea from your thesis statement can be an effective way to start brainstorming a title. Here are some alternative titles for Essay 2.1:

Use a question:	What Are the Dangers of Texting While Driving?
Start with *-ing* form:	Texting While Driving: The Dangers
Include an adjective:	The Dangerous Trend of Texting While Driving
Use only one or two words:	Dangerous Driving

ACTIVITY 10 | Proofreading a paragraph

Read the teacher's comments on a student's final draft of a paragraph. Then rewrite the paragraph on a separate piece of paper.

PARAGRAPH 2.2

title?
_____

spelling

Learning nouns in a new <u>langugue</u> may seem easy, but in fact the grammar of nouns

language

can vary from language to language. Spanish, for example, has male nouns and female nouns,

but why *newspaper* is masculine and *magazine* is feminine is a mystery. Japanese nouns

have no plural form, so Japanese learners of English may think *-s* is unnecessary in the

phrase *many books* because the word *many* already means plural. <u>In German, all nouns are</u>

combine sentences   wrong connector

<u>capitalized. English capitalizes nouns that name specific people, places, and things.</u> <u>Therefore,</u>

avoid contraction

English <u>doesn't</u> capitalize *woman* or *city*, but it does capitalize *Susan* and *Cairo*. Finally, some

languages mark the role of the noun as subject or direct object, so in Japanese, *-wa* is often

word form

<u>add</u> to a noun as subject and *-o* to a noun as the direct object of a verb. English does not

article

require suffixes to mark the role of nouns in <u>sentence</u>. Because nouns express basic ideas such

as the name of a person, place, or thing, they seem easy, but they can be confusing.

Grammar: Subject-Verb Agreement

In any sentence, the subject and verb must agree in number.

EXPLANATION	EXAMPLES
A singular verb must be used with a singular subject. A plural verb must be used with a plural subject.	An important **export is** cocoa. Important **exports are** cocoa and palm oil.
The object of a preposition is never the subject of a sentence. Words that come between the subject and the verb can sometimes cause writers to choose the wrong number for the verb.	✓ The main **export** of <u>some Central American countries</u> **is** coffee. ✗ The main **export** of <u>some Central American countries</u> **are** coffee. ✓ The main **exports** of <u>Guatemala</u> **are** coffee, sugar, and bananas. ✗ The main **exports** of <u>Guatemala</u> **is** coffee, sugar, and bananas.

ACTIVITY 11 | Practicing subject-verb agreement

Write the correct form of the verb in parentheses.

1. After tragic events, people often (react) _____React_____ quite differently.

2. NATO (consist) _____consists_____ of 29 member states.

3. Of all the surveys regarding people's daily habits that were conducted last year, two in particular (stand out) _____stand out_____ as examples of good survey methods.

4. The primary cause of global warming (be) _____is_____ human activity.

5. Vietnam (have) _____has_____ a very interesting history.

6. The largest countries in South America (be) _____are_____ Brazil and Argentina.

A polar bear hangs on to an ice floe in Svalbard, Norway.

7. The ingredients in this soup (be) _____ are _____ listed on the can.

8. The life cycle of the butterfly, from egg to larva to chrysalis to adult, (provide)

    _____ provides _____ a vivid example of the complexity of nature.

9. Both face-to-face and online courses (share) _____ share _____ the same goal.

10. Another way to increase people's sense of personal happiness (involve)

    _____ involves _____ their perception of job satisfaction.

ACTIVITY 12 | Practicing with subject-verb agreement

Fill in the blank with the correct form of the verb in parentheses.

PARAGRAPH 2.3

Aziz Abu Sarah in Cambodia

Aziz Abu Sarah [1] _____ is _____ (be) a National Geographic Explorer and cultural educator. His work [2] _____ center _____ (center) on conflict resolution. In particular, he looks for ways to build bridges between groups of people that [3] _____ have _____ (have) historically been separated. He [4] _____ uses _____ (use) stories and cross-cultural learning to foster understanding in order to generate positive social change. During the 2014 World Cup Finals in Brazil, Aziz reflected on the way sports [5] _____ promote _____ (promote) unity and cross-cultural learning. While the media often [6] _____ portrays _____ (portray) an image of destructive or violent fans, Aziz witnessed goodwill among spectators from different nations. Aziz and a business partner [7] _____ are _____ (be) the founders of MEJDI Tours, a company that [8] _____ sends _____ (send) tourists to different parts of the world to experience first-hand how the people in these places actually [9] _____ live _____. (live) Putting tourists in direct contact with locals not only [10] _____ helps _____ (help) to break down stereotypes but also [11] _____ promotes _____ (promote) understanding, friendship, and peace.

BUILDING BETTER VOCABULARY

WORDS TO KNOW

anticipate (v) AW
at once (adv)
bargain (v) AW
demonstrate (v) AW
desire (n)
harm (n)
interchangeable (adj)

maximize (v)
minor (adj) AW
multitask (v) AW
negotiable (adj)
occupational (adj)
rational (adj) AW
shift (v) AW

strategize (v)
thereby (adv) AW
tough (adj) AW
tragic (adj)
up to (adv)
virtually (adv) AW

ACTIVITY 13 | Word associations

Circle the word or phrase that is most closely related to the word or phrase on the left.

1. anticipate	expect	increase
2. at once	correctly	immediately
3. bargain	win	deal
4. desire	purpose	want
5. minor	less interesting	less important
6. occupational	work	play
7. shift	accept	change
8. thereby	as a result	in order to
9. tragic	colorful	sad
10. virtually	nearly	graphically

ACTIVITY 14 | Collocations

Fill in the blank with the word or phrase that most naturally completes the phrase.

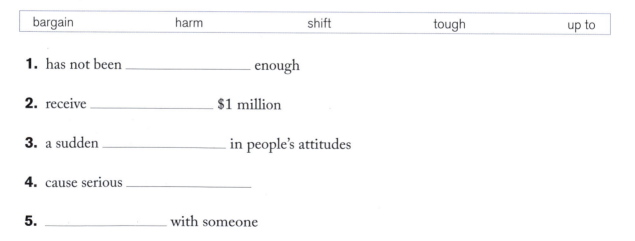

bargain	harm	shift	tough	up to

1. has not been _____ enough

2. receive _____ $1 million

3. a sudden _____ in people's attitudes

4. cause serious _____

5. _____ with someone

| desire | minor | multitask | occupational | rational |

6. a(n) _____ hazard

7. an ability to _____

8. a(n) _____ mind

9. a deep _____ to learn

10. a(n) _____ concern

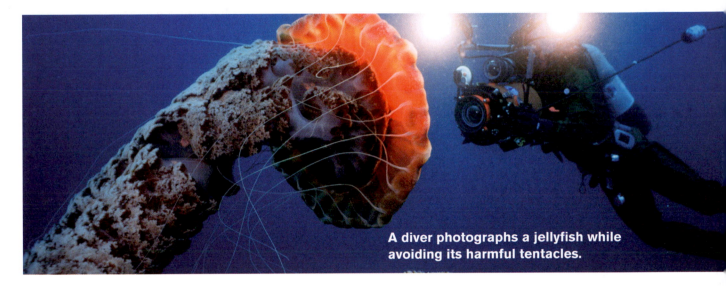

A diver photographs a jellyfish while avoiding its harmful tentacles.

ACTIVITY 15 | Word forms

Complete each sentence with the correct word form. Use the correct form of the verbs.

NOUN	VERB	ADJECTIVE	ADVERB	SENTENCES
harm	harm	harmful		**1.** Too much sunlight can be very _harmful_ to your health. **2.** What is the _harm_ in having a break every so often?
maximum	maximize	maximized maximum		**3.** At some hotels, a _____ of three guests can stay in the same room. **4.** What is the best strategy to _____ the funds for your retirement?
negotiation	negotiate	negotiable		**5.** At the end of the _____, each side got the result that it wanted. **6.** For most parents, bedtime curfews are not _____.

shift	shift	shifting		**7.** A _____ in public opinion has happened because of bad news reports. **8.** The wind suddenly _____ direction, making it hard to climb the hill.
tragedy		tragic	tragically	**9.** _____, no one survived the plane crash. **10.** It is a _____ that she lost all of her home in the flood.

ACTIVITY 16 | Vocabulary in writing

Choose five words from Words to Know. Write a complete sentence with each word.

1. _____

2. _____

3. _____

4. _____

5. _____

BUILDING BETTER SENTENCES

ACTIVITY 17 | Editing

Each sentence has two errors. Find and correct them.

1. Sometimes a word can be more than one part of speech with no change at all, but other time the ending of the word changes to indicate whether is a noun, verb, adjective, or adverb.

2. A roller coaster is a type of the amusement park attraction with a railroad system where cars can to travel up and down slopes at fast speeds.

3. The country of Switzerland lie in the center of Europe, while Norway and Greece is at the extremes of the continent.

4. Jambalaya is dish from Louisiana that people make it with rice, vegetables, and seafood.

5. Texting and driving can have tragedy results, so it is best don't look at a phone at all when operating a car.

ACTIVITY 18 | Writing sentences

Read the pairs of words. Write an original sentence using the words listed.

1. (anticipate/tough)

_____

2. (desire/rational)

_____

3. (multitask/up to)

_____

4. (bargain/maximize)

_____

5. (minor/negotiable)

_____

ACTIVITY 19 | Combining sentences

Combine the ideas into one sentence. You may change the word forms, but do not change or omit any ideas. There may be more than one answer.

1. Owning a car is expensive.
In Vietnam, it is very expensive.
This is because of a high government tax.
Therefore, there are many more motorcycles than cars.

_____

_____

2. Rabbits are natural runners.
They can run at 30 mph.
They can reach speeds 40 mph.

_____

_____

3. The highest score in a World Cup game occurred in 1954.
Austria defeated Switzerland in the quarterfinal.
The score was 7–5.

_____

_____

WRITING

In this section, you will follow the seven steps in the writing process to write an essay.

ACTIVITY 20 | Following the writing process.

Step 1: Choose a topic

Choose a topic for your essay. Your teacher may assign a topic, you may think of one yourself, or you may choose one from the chart below. Then answer the questions.

1. What topic did you choose? _____

2. Why did you choose this topic? _____

3. How well do you know this topic? What is your experience with it? _____

_____

Humanities	*Linguistics:* How difficult is it to learn English compared to learning another language? *Literature:* Some people think that the *Harry Potter* books revived interest in reading in both adults and children. Write an essay that offers three reasons to support this claim.
Sciences	What is global warming? What can be done to slow this process down?
Business	Many new businesses fail in their first three years of operation. What are the characteristics of a successful new business?
Personal	In your opinion, what are the three most important qualities of a good sibling? Explain why each of these qualities is necessary for your definition of a good sibling.

Step 2: Brainstorm

On a separate piece of paper, write as many ideas about your topic as you can. Use a mind map or T-chart if appropriate.

Step 3: Outline

Using the ideas from Step 2, write an outline of your essay. Then exchange your outline with a partner. Use the Peer Editing Form 1 for Outlines in the *Writer's Handbook* to help you comment on your partner's work. Use your partner's feedback to revise your outline.

Step 4: Write the first draft

Use your outline and the feedback received to write the first draft of your essay.

Step 5: Get feedback from a peer

Exchange your first draft with a partner. Use Peer Editing Form 2 in the *Writer's Handbook* to help you comment on your partner's writing.

Step 6: Reread, rethink, rewrite

Read the comments from your peer editor. Identify places where you could make revisions. Then write as many drafts as necessary to improve your essay. Remember to proofread your essay before you submit it so that you correct any errors.

Step 7: Write a final draft

Additional Topics for Writing

Here are five more ideas for writing an essay.

TOPIC 1: Look at the photo below. Think about an adventure that you have had. Were you alone? What happened? Describe your experience.

TOPIC 2: What are the effects of daily exercise?

TOPIC 3: Explain how to make a pizza.

TOPIC 4: Explain the benefits or inconveniences of travel.

TOPIC 5: Should the government sponsor lotteries? Why or why not?

TEST PREP

Write an essay about the following topic. You should spend about 40 minutes on this task.

Some people believe that all students should study a foreign language before they can graduate. Others do not support this requirement. Write an essay in which you agree with one of these two positions.

Include a short introduction with a thesis statement, three body paragraphs, and a brief conclusion. Remember to proofread your essay.

TIP

Be aware of the time limit on a writing test. Assume you want at least 10 minutes to review your writing, so you should subtract 10 minutes from the total time to determine the time for writing. For example, if the time limit is 40 minutes, this means you really have about 30 minutes to write.

Bikers cross the Kali Gandaki suspension bridge in Nepal.

OBJECTIVES
- Learn how to paraphrase, summarize, and synthesize
- Learn how to cite information from sources
- Know when to paraphrase and when to use direct quotations
- Write an essay that synthesizes information

Using Original Sources

Greg Anderson and David Harrison of the Living Tongues Institute for Endangered Languages interview Dorji Khandu Thongdok and Lam Norbu, Sherdukpen speakers in India, as part of their research to document and preserve endangered languages.

FREEWRITE | Look at the photo and read the caption. On a separate piece of paper write what you think are the characteristics of a good source of information.

ELEMENTS OF GREAT WRITING

Using Information from Original Sources

The majority of the words in an essay should be written by you and not by someone else. Sometimes, however, you may want to use an idea from an outside source—a book, a website, an interview, a journal, and so on—to support your statements. In fact, readers actually *expect* information from outside sources to support key points or ideas. This expectation is so strong that not using outside information can make your paper less convincing. Including outside sources shows that you have considered existing ideas before proposing a new idea in your essay.

Avoiding Plagiarism

If you use an original source in your paper but do not cite it, the reader will assume the information is yours. Whether you do this intentionally or accidentally, letting your reader think information is yours when it is not is considered academic dishonesty, or **plagiarism**. If you do not give credit for borrowed ideas or words, you are guilty of academic theft, and such stealing of ideas or words is not tolerated. It is not acceptable to use even a few words from another source without citing the source. Whether you take one sentence, one paragraph, or one chapter, it is stealing. To avoid this academic offense, you need to acknowledge the owner of the original information.

Adding Citations

Because words and ideas from outside sources are not yours, it is necessary to indicate the author's name and the date his/her work appeared in a publication. This is called **citing**—sources cited in an essay are called **citations**.

Note that facts considered to be general knowledge and found in many places, such as "Paris is the largest city in France," can be freely used in your writing without citing a source. However, when a paper uses information that is not generally known and comes from one particular source, then the author needs to list which sources were used.

ACTIVITY 1 | Recognizing kinds of information

Read the different kinds of information. Write *NC* for general information that would NOT need a citation in an essay or *C* for information that would need a citation.

1. _____ **a.** The date given in several encyclopedias when the first *Star Wars* movie was released in the United States.

   _____ **b.** A quote from a magazine interview with director George Lucas about the release of the first *Star Wars* movie.

2. _____ **a.** A description of the architectural styles evident in the temples of Angkor Wat given in a magazine article.

   _____ **b.** Facts from tourist guides about who built Angkor Wat.

3. _____ **a.** The date from an encyclopedia when physicist Marie Curie won the Nobel.

   _____ **b.** A report about Curie's Nobel Prize ceremony included in a biography of Marie Curie.

4. _____ **a.** Key dates, people, and places involved in the discovery of Chauvet Cave, the site of prehistoric drawings.

_____ **b.** An art historian's interpretation of the drawings at Chauvet Cave.

Four Ways to Use Information from Original Sources

There are four main ways to include information from an original source in your essay:

1. Direct Quotation

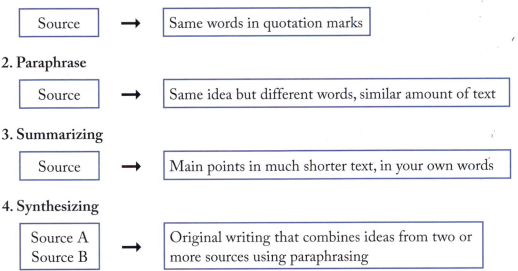

2. Paraphrase

3. Summarizing

4. Synthesizing

Using Direct Quotation and Paraphrasing

When you find information to support the claims of your essay, either use the exact words you have found (**direct quotation**) or include the information in your own words (**paraphrase**).

Compare the direct quotations and the paraphrases in these examples:

DIRECT QUOTATION	PARAPHRASING
According to a well-known comment by Wilkins (1972), "While without grammar very little can be conveyed, without vocabulary nothing can be conveyed" (p. 111).	Wilkins (1972) indicated that vocabulary is more important than grammar in communication.
In her report of the financial status of the company, Chief Financial Officer Maria Simpson said, "Despite the fact that we are a relatively new and small company, last year we sold more than 22 million phones, once again wildly exceeding our pre-year forecast. We are and expect to remain very profitable in the next five years."	Chief Financial Officer Maria Simpson is optimistic about the company's financial situation for the next five years. In her report, she noted that the company did much better than predicted and sold over 22 million phones last year.

Notice how paraphrasing includes the same idea or message as the direct quotation, but the wording of the direct quotation makes a stronger impression on the reader. For example, using the exact words in the quotation by Maria Simpson sounds more persuasive.

Paraphrasing

Paraphrasing is a difficult skill because it involves using different words and structures to communicate the same idea as another writer. Follow the steps below to paraphrase effectively:

STEPS TO WRITING PARAPHRASES
1. Read and understand the source material. 2. Keep the main idea(s) of the information that you want to use. 3. Think of a different way to present that information. 4. Use different vocabulary. 5. Use different sentence and grammatical structures. 6. Make sure the new paraphrase sounds like your writing.

Imagine you wanted to paraphrase this sentence from an article written by Dave Thio in 2017:

Selling a product successfully in another country often requires changes in the product.

First, you would note that the main idea is that companies should change their products to succeed in another country. Now, study an example of a good paraphrase and one of a poor paraphrase.

GOOD PARAPHRASE	POOR PARAPHRASE
Thio (2017) suggests that companies that market products well usually do so by making changes in their products. ✓ It keeps the idea that change is necessary. ✓ Grammar is different (subject: *companies;* verb: *do;* dependent clause: *that market products well*). ✓ Vocabulary is different (*companies, market*).	*Thio (2017) suggests that to sell a product successfully in another country, you often need to change the product.* ✗ The ideas are the same, but the wording is too similar (*successfully, in another country*). This is plagiarism. ✗ Only minor changes were made (*selling = to sell; often requires = you need to*). ✗ The use of *you* is usually not acceptable in academic writing.

Green Kit Kat and other chocolates on sale in Tokyo, Japan

ACTIVITY 2 | Identifying examples of good paraphrasing

Read the paragraph. Highlight the most important ideas in the two sentences that are underlined. Then read the paraphrases on the next page. Write *TS* if the paraphrase is too similar, *X* for a paraphrase that has a different meaning or wrong information, and *P* for the best paraphrase.

WORDS TO KNOW Paragraph 3.1

array: (n) a large group
found: (v) to create or establish

intensive: (adj) fast; concentrated

PARAGRAPH 3.1

Orlando: From Tiny Town to Major City

The city of Orlando, located in sunny central Florida, has experienced enormous growth and is internationally known as a popular tourist destination. **Founded** in 1844, Orlando was a small town for more than a century. With the arrival of the South Florida Railroad in 1880, Orlando was on its way to **intensive** growth. This growth increased with the development of the Cape Canaveral space center in 1950. Two decades later, Orlando experienced rapid growth again on an incredible scale when Walt Disney World opened its gates to tourists in 1971. Located 22 miles (35 kilometers) southwest of Orlando, the Disney area alone covers some 28,000 acres[1]. In addition to having Florida's largest hotel, Walt Disney World has an **array** of thrilling attractions, including the Magic Kingdom, Epcot, Disney's Hollywood Studios, and Animal Kingdom. With an increase in tourism, the metropolitan[2] area of Orlando has undergone an amazing amount of growth.

[1]acre: a measurement of land 69.57 yards (63.57 meters) on each side
[2]metropolitan: related to a city and its suburbs

Visitors at a space exhibit in Walt Disney World, Orlando

1. With the arrival of the South Florida Railroad in 1880, Orlando was on its way to intensive growth.

    _____ **a.** With the arrival of the South Florida Railroad in 1880, the city of Orlando was on its way to fast growth.

    _____ **b.** Most people were genuinely shocked at how quickly Orlando grew after the South Florida Railroad arrived in 1880.

    _____ **c.** The city of Orlando began to grow tremendously when the South Florida Railroad reached the city in 1880.

2. Two decades later, Orlando experienced rapid growth again on an incredible scale when Walt Disney World opened its gates to tourists in 1971.

    _____ **a.** Twenty years later, Orlando saw rapid growth again when Walt Disney World opened for tourists in 1971.

    _____ **b.** In 1971, Orlando again grew tremendously with the arrival of Walt Disney World.

    _____ **c.** Walt Disney World began in Orlando in 1971, and the park attracted more than 20 times more tourists than any other Florida site.

ACTIVITY 3 | Writing paraphrases

Highlight the most important idea(s) in each sentence. Then write a paraphrase.

1. Located 22 miles southwest of Orlando, the Disney area alone covers some 28,000 acres.

    Approximately 28000 acres compose the Disney resort which is 22 miles southwest of Orlando

2. In addition to having Florida's largest hotel, Walt Disney World has an array of thrilling attractions, including the Magic Kingdom, Epcot, Disney's Hollywood Studios, and Animal Kingdom.

    _____

    _____

    _____

Writing Direct Quotations

While paraphrasing is the more common way to use other people's ideas in your writing, you may find a sentence or phrase that you want to quote directly without changing the original language. Direct quotations can be used when the original language is strong or eloquent and provides a particularly powerful way to express the idea. A direct quotation should not be more than two or three lines. Longer direct quotations require special treatment and are not common in essays. They are more commonly used in research papers. Also, your essay should have only a few direct quotations. Do not let other writers drown out your voice and ideas.

Just as with paraphrasing, it is always necessary to cite the original writer and source of the information. To do this, you should use an introductory phrase such as *According to* (original writer or source) or (Original writer or source) *reports that*.

Methods of Citing Sources

Two of the most commonly used methods for citing works are **APA** (American Psychology Association) and **MLA** (Modern Language Association). In general, APA is used in the sciences and social sciences, while MLA is used in the humanities. They are fairly similar, so learning to use one will make it easy to learn the second one if it is needed later.

In this book, the examples in Units 1, 2, 3, 4, 6, and 8 use APA, and the examples in Units 5 and 7 use MLA. When you write a research paper for a class, you should confirm with the instructor which method to use for your paper: APA or MLA. (For a more detailed overview of MLA and APA citation, see the *Writer's Handbook*.)

In-Text Citation Format

When using a direct quotation from a book in APA style, you must state the last name of the author, the date of the publication, and the page number(s) of the direct quotation. When you paraphrase, usually only the author and date are required. Look at the examples below and notice the placement, style, and format of the citation.

APA Style

DIRECT QUOTATION	PARAPHRASE
According to Coxhead (2017), "In an international school context, learners are expected to be able to cope with the English language, the subject content, and the educational context at the same time" (p. 229).	Coxhead (2017) suggests that, in addition to English, these learners must master the subject being taught as well as navigate a foreign school system (p. 229).
She stated, "In an international school context, learners are expected to be able to cope with the English language, the subject content, and the educational context at the same time" (Coxhead, 2017, p. 229).	In addition to English, these learners must master the subject being taught as well as navigate a foreign school system (Coxhead, 2017, p. 229).

In MLA style, you must state the name of the author and the page number(s) for a direct quotation and paraphrase. Look at the examples below and notice the placement, style, and format of the citation.

MLA Style

DIRECT QUOTATION	PARAPHRASE
According to Coxhead, "In an international school context, learners are expected to be able to cope with the English language, the subject content, and the educational context at the same time" (229).	Coxhead notes, in addition to English, these learners must master the subject being taught as well as navigate a foreign school system (229).
She stated, "In an international school context, learners are expected to be able to cope with the English language, the subject content, and the educational context at the same time" (Coxhead, 229).	In addition to English, these learners must master the subject being taught as well as navigate a foreign school system (Coxhead, 229).

ACTIVITY 4 | Adding in-text citations

Use "According to" to introduce correct in-text citation of the direct quote in 1 and of the paraphrase in 2. The original source is from page 111 of a book by David A. Wilkins called *Linguistics in Language Teaching* published in 1972.

1. "While without grammar very little can be conveyed, without vocabulary nothing can be conveyed."

    a. APA: According to Wilkins (1972), " " (p.111)

    b. MLA: According to Wilkins, " " (111)

2. Communication depends much more on vocabulary than on grammar.

    a. APA:

    b. MLA: Wilkins notes, communication depends much more on vocabulary than on grammar (111)

End of Essay Citation Format

Every source cited within an essay is also included in a list at the end of the essay. In APA, this end-of-essay section is labeled "References" whereas in MLA it is called "Works Cited." In both MLA and APA, sources are listed in alphabetical order by the author's last name.

Note the formatting and punctuation used in APA and MLA style for a book citation:

APA

Last name, Initial(s). (Publication year). *Title of Book*. City and State (or country) of publication: Publisher.

Hale, K., Montjoy, R., & Brown, M. (2015). *Administering elections: How American elections work*. New York: Palgrave Macmillan.

MLA

Last Name, First Name. *Title of Book*. Publisher, Publication year.

Hale, Kathleen, Robert Montjoy, and Mitchell Brown. *Administering Elections: How American Elections Work*. Palgrave Macmillan, 2015.

ACTIVITY 5 | Writing end-of-essay citations

Write an APA and MLA citation for the book by David A. Wilkins called *Linguistics in Language Teaching* published in 1972 by a publisher in London called Edward Arnold.

1. References

David A., W.,   (1972) Linguistics in language Teaching. London: Edward Aarnold

2. Works Cited

Introducing a Direct Quotation or a Paraphrase

> **WORDS TO KNOW**
>
> **acute:** (adj) severe
> **concede:** (v) to admit that something is true
> **point out:** (phr v) to indicate
>
> **reveal:** (v) to show something hidden
> **seek:** (v) to look for (past = sought)

One of the most common ways to introduce a direct quotation or a paraphrase is to use the preposition *according to* (+ kind or name of publication) + *by* (name of author/s).

> According to a report by Tinsley (2018), "Senior citizens who have experienced **acute** chest pains at least twice in the past six months often find themselves back in the hospital within a month if they have not **sought** professional treatment" (p. 37).

> According to Tinsley (2018), elderly patients who have suffered severe chest pains more than once in six months should get medical treatment or they may require serious medical treatment again within 30 days (p. 37).

You can also use academic reporting verbs such as *suggest*, *report*, *indicate* (+ *that*):

Poundstone (2017) suggests, "Where possible, give a good answer that the interviewer has never encountered before" (p. 129).

Poundstone (2017) indicates that the originality of an answer during an interview can lead to a successful outcome (p. 129).

Note that the verb introducing a citation can be in the simple past or simple present tense. It is common to use simple present tense when the information is still applicable today. However, some academic fields prefer one tense over the other. Here are some common reporting verbs:

admit (to)	disagree (with)	maintain	predict	show
agree (with)	explain	note	propose	suggest
concede	find	observe	report	think
conclude	insist	**point out**	**reveal**	warn

ACTIVITY 6 | Using reporting verbs with direct quotations

Paraphrase each direct quotation using a different reporting verb to introduce each.

1. "Many of life's failures are people who did not realize how close they were to success when they gave up."—Thomas Edison

    _____

    _____

2. "Twenty years from now you will be more disappointed by the things that you didn't do than by the ones you did do."—Mark Twain

    _____

    _____

3. "Peace of mind is the mental condition in which you have accepted the worst."—Lin Yutang

    _____

    _____

4. "The most common way people give up their power is thinking they don't have any."—Alice Walker

    _____

    _____

5. "Life is far too important of a thing ever to talk seriously about it."—Oscar Wilde

    _____

    _____

Summarizing

Another way to include information from an original source is by **summarizing** it. Summarizing is especially useful when you are taking information from longer sources. When summarizing, do not include all of the information from the source. Instead, use only the parts you think are important. Remember that summaries do not contain any of your original ideas.

A summary is always shorter than the original piece. A 10-page article might become a few paragraphs in a summary. A 200-page book might be summarized in a short essay.

STEPS TO WRITING A SUMMARY
1. Read the source material and understand it well.
2. Decide which ideas or pieces of information in the source material are the most important.
3. Paraphrase each idea using different grammar and vocabulary.
4. Connect the paraphrased ideas together in the same order they appear in the original.

ACTIVITY 7 | Understanding summarizing

Read Paragraph 3.2. Then compare and discuss the two examples of summarizing.

WORDS TO KNOW Paragraph 3.2

premium: (adj) higher quality   **without a doubt:** (phr) with certainty

---

PARAGRAPH 3.2 **APA**

Selling a Domestic Product Overseas

Selling a product successfully in another country often requires changes in the product, as Pride, Hughes, and Kapoor (2014) explain using specific products from three well-known American companies that attempted to expand internationally. Domino's Pizza offers mayonnaise and potato pizza in Tokyo and pickled ginger pizza in India. Heinz varies its ketchup recipe to satisfy the needs of specific markets. In Belgium and Holland, for example, the ketchup is not as sweet as it is in the United States. When Häagen-Dazs served up one of its most popular American flavors, Chocolate Chip Cookie Dough, to British customers, they left it sitting in supermarket freezers. What the **premium** ice-cream maker learned is that chocolate chip cookies are not popular in Great Britain, and children do not have a history of snatching raw dough from the bowl. As a result, the company had to develop flavors that would sell in Great Britain. Because dairy products are not part of Chinese diets, Frito-Lay took the cheese out of Cheetos in China. Instead, the company sells Seafood Cheetos. **Without a doubt**, these products were successful in these foreign lands only because the company realized that it was wise to do market research and make fundamental changes in the products.

Reference

Pride, W. M., Hughes, R. J., & Kapoor, J. R. (2014). *Business* (12th ed.). Mason, Ohio: South-Western Cengage Learning.

GOOD SUMMARY	POOR SUMMARY
Companies must adapt their products if they want to do well in foreign markets. Many well-known companies, including Domino's, Heinz, Häagen-Dazs, and Frito-Lay, have altered their products and proved this point.	Changes in a product are important if a company wants to sell it successfully in another country. For example, Domino's Pizza offers mayonnaise and potato pizza in Tokyo. Heinz changed its ketchup. When Häagen-Dazs served one of its popular American flavors, Chocolate Chip Cookie Dough, to British customers, the customers left it sitting in supermarkets. The ice-cream maker learned that chocolate chip cookies are not popular in Great Britain, and children do not eat uncooked dough. As a result, the company developed flavors to sell in Great Britain. Certainly, these items were successful in these countries because the company was smart enough to do market research and implement changes in the products.
✓ It covers the main ideas.	✗ It is long and, therefore, not really a summary.
✓ It is a true summary, not an exact repeat of the specific examples.	✗ It includes almost the same vocabulary, for example: "*left it sitting in supermarket freezers*" versus "*left it sitting in supermarkets.*" This is plagiarism.
✓ It includes some new grammar, for example: *often requires changes* versus *companies must adapt.*	✗ It includes almost the same grammar, for example: "*As a result, the company had to develop flavors that would sell in Great Britain.*" versus "*As a result, the company developed flavors to sell in Great Britain.*" This is plagiarism.
✓ It includes some new vocabulary.	

An ice cream parlor in London, UK

ACTIVITY 8 | Paraphrasing key information

Write a paraphrase of each of the four underlined segments.

> **WORDS TO KNOW** Paragraph 3.3
>
> **commercialism:** (n) a focus on profit-making **congestion:** (n) a condition of overcrowding

PARAGRAPH 3.3

The Effects of Tourism on One Florida City

Orlando, which was a quiet farming town a little more than 50 years ago, has more people passing through it than any other place in the state of Florida. The reason, of course, is Walt Disney World, Universal Studios, Sea World, and many other attractions. These theme parks pull more than 55 million people a year to what was until relatively recently an empty area of land. Few of these people visit the actual city of Orlando. Instead, they prefer to stay in one of the countless motels fifteen miles to the south along Highway 19 or five miles southwest on International Drive. Despite enormous expansion over the last two decades, the city itself remains free of the **commercialism** that surrounds it. However, the city has not been able to escape the traffic **congestion** and other problems associated with the visit of so many millions of tourists as well as the thousands of people who work in the tourist industry. Without a doubt, tourism has changed life for the residents of Orlando and the surrounding area.

1. _____

_____

2. _____

_____

3. _____

_____

4. _____

_____

ACTIVITY 9 | Writing a summary

Use your paraphrases from Activity 8 and other information that you think is important to write a summary of Paragraph 3.3. Write on a separate piece of paper.

Synthesizing

A **synthesis** is a combination of information from two or more sources. When synthesizing, take information from different sources and blend them smoothly into your paragraph.

STEPS TO WRITING A SYNTHESIS
1. Read the material from all of the sources.
2. Choose the important information from each source.
3. Group together the ideas that are connected and that support each other.
4. Combine the ideas in each group into sentences, using your paraphrasing skills.
5. Organize the sentences logically and combine them into one continuous piece of writing.

ACTIVITY 10 | Understanding synthesis

Read Paragraphs A and B. Then compare and discuss the syntheses on the next page.

WORDS TO KNOW Paragraphs A and B	
fraction: (n) a part	**linguistic:** (adj) related to languages

PARAGRAPH A

   Switzerland is a great example of **linguistic** diversity because three main languages are widely spoken there. People in the central and northern areas speak mostly German. People in the western area usually speak French. People in the southeastern area of the country speak mostly Italian. Many Swiss can speak morea than one language. One interesting fact is that the name of the country on its coins and stamps is not in any of these languages. Instead, "Helvetia," the Latin name for this country, is used.

PARAGRAPH B

   You might think that most of the people in Switzerland speak the same language because it is a rather small country. However, you would be wrong. Yes, the country is tiny, yet Switzerland has four official languages. German is spoken by more people than any other language. The second most commonly spoken language is French, and Italian is third. Only a tiny **fraction** of the population speaks Romansch.

GOOD SYNTHESIS	POOR SYNTHESIS
Although Switzerland is a small country, several languages are spoken there. In fact, it has four national languages. The most commonly spoken language is German, which is used in the central and northern regions. The second most widely spoken language is French, which is used in the western area of the country. The third is Italian, which is spoken in the southeast. A fourth language, Romansch, is spoken by a small percentage of the population. Ironically, the name for Switzerland on Swiss currency is not in any of these languages. Instead, "Helvetia," the Latin term for this country, is used.	Switzerland is not big, but there are four national languages. The languages in order of usage are: German, French, Italian, and Romansch. Portuguese and Greek are not spoken. People in the western area speak French. People in the southeastern area of the country speak Italian. People in the central and northern areas speak German. One interesting fact is that the name of the country on its coins and stamps is not in any of these languages. Instead, "Helvetia," the Latin name, is used.
✓ It has ideas from both sources (for example, Source A: *German is spoken in central and northern regions;* Source B: *the most common language is German*).	✗ The ideas are not woven together well. It is easy to see where one source ends and the other begins. Source B ends after *The languages in order of usage are German, French, Italian, and Romansch.* Source A takes up the rest of the paragraph.
✓ The ideas are woven together. (*The most commonly spoken language is German, which is used in the central and northern regions.*).	✗ The third sentence is an unrelated idea about Portuguese and Greek that is not from either source.
✓ The sequence of the material is logical (first, second, third, fourth most common languages).	✗ The sequence of the languages by geographical areas is illogical; it does not match the list of languages at the beginning of the paragraph.

ACTIVITY 11 | Writing a synthesis

Read these two paragraphs about Julia Child. Underline important information in each. Then write one paragraph on a separate piece of paper that synthesizes the information from both.

> **WORDS TO KNOW** Paragraphs A and B
>
> **complex**: (adj) difficult
> **legacy**: (n) something handed down from the past
>
> **master**: (v) to learn how to do something well
> **pioneer**: (n) a person who leads the way for others into a new area of knowledge or invention

PARAGRAPH A

Julia Child, born in 1912, became internationally famous in the 1960s with the publication of her cookbook, *Mastering the Art of French Cooking*. The book was praised for its sharp attention to detail, step-by-step instructions, and clear illustrations of **complex** cooking techniques. Over the remainder of her life, Child published approximately 20 more books, including her autobiography, *My Life in France*. Today's celebrity chefs owe a debt of gratitude to Julia Child, an early **pioneer** of the field.

A world-renowned chef, Julia Child became famous for her first cookbook, *Mastering the Art of French Cooking*, and she cemented her celebrity status with several television programs, including *Julia Child & Company* and *Dinner at Julia's*. In several of her early programs, before television shows could be easily edited, she made mistakes in her preparations, resulting in failed dishes. Ironically, her mistakes endeared her to her audience, as she demonstrated that even great chefs have bad days. Child died in 2004, leaving behind her a lasting **legacy** of delicious food.

BUILDING BETTER VOCABULARY

WORDS TO KNOW

acute (adj) AW	found (v)	pioneer (n)
array (n) AW	fraction (n) AW	point out (phr v)
commercialism (n)	intensive (adj) AW	premium (adj)
complex (adj) AW	legacy (n)	reveal (v) AW
concede (v)	linguistic (adj) AW	seek (v)
congestion (n)	master (v)	without a doubt (phr)

ACTIVITY 12 | Word associations

Circle the word or phrase that is more closely related to the word on the left.

1. acute	severe	wonderful
2. array	assignment	choices
3. complex	complicated	contrary
4. concede	claim you are right	admit you are wrong
5. congestion	a lot of free time	a lot of people
6. found	finish	start
7. fraction	a part	a person
8. premium	higher quality	lower quality
9. reveal	hate	show
10. seek	look for	listen to

ACTIVITY 13 | Collocations

Fill in the blank with the word or phrase that most naturally completes the phrase.

array	concede	legacy	pioneer	point out

1. _____ an election

2. a wide _____ of

3. a lasting _____

4. an early _____

5. _____ differences

complex	congestion	fraction	intensive	reveal

6. a small _____ of the population

7. _____ training

8. bad _____ on the roads

9. a(n) _____ problem

10. _____ a secret

ACTIVITY 14 | Word forms

Complete each sentence with the correct word form. Use the correct form of the verbs.

NOUN	VERB	ADJECTIVE	ADVERB	SENTENCES
		acute	acutely	**1.** There is an _____ traffic problem here.
				2. _____ ill patients need special care.
commercialism	commercialize	commercial	commercially	**3.** The United States is known for its _____.
				4. The medicine is not _____ available yet.
complexity		complex		**5.** No one was able to solve the _____ math problem.
				6. The _____ of the human brain is unparalleled.

NOUN	VERB	ADJECTIVE	ADVERB	SENTENCES
intensity	intensify	intensive intensified intensifying	intensively	**7.** A good way to learn English is to enroll in an _____ program because there are classes every day. **8.** This app _____ the colors in a photo.
mastery	master	masterful	masterfully	**9.** It takes a long time to _____ a new language. **10.** Full _____ of a new language can take years, depending on the learner.

ACTIVITY 15 | Vocabulary in writing

Choose five words from Words to Know. Write a complete sentence with each word.

1. _____

2. _____

3. _____

4. _____

5. _____

Barrington Irving is a pioneer—he was the first African American to fly solo around the world.

BUILDING BETTER SENTENCES

ACTIVITY 16 | Editing

Each sentence has two errors. Find and correct them.

1. Due to the numerous factory in that area, the quality of the air in that regional of the country is quite poor.

2. According the article, the largest states are Alaska, Texas, and Montana, but Alaska and Montana has relatively small populations.

3. Unlike just twenty years ago, obtain a good job today require social networking skills.

4. An important question for consider is whether schools with smaller class sizes produces better test scores.

5. Some airline officials who were early advocates for purchase the new aircraft have recently complain about the lack of training for crew members.

ACTIVITY 17 | Combining sentences

Combine the ideas into one sentence. You may change the word forms, but do not change or omit any ideas. There is more than one answer.

1. Badgers have short legs for digging.
   Badgers can run surprisingly fast.
   They can run up to 30 kph.
   They can only run so fast for a short period of time.

   _____

   _____

   _____

2. The famous composer Ludwig van Beethoven lost his hearing.
   He lost his hearing in 1801.
   Beethoven completed many of his most famous works around 1820.
   These works include his ninth symphony.

   _____

   _____

   _____

3. Venus is the second planet from the sun.
Venus is named for a Roman goddess.
She was the Roman goddess of love and beauty.
The average temperature on Venus is 462 degrees Celsius.

_____

_____

_____

ACTIVITY 18 | Writing sentences

Read the pairs of words. Write an original sentence using the words listed.

1. (society/commercialism) _____

_____

2. (acute/problem) _____

_____

3. (report/reveal) _____

_____

4. (without a doubt/thrilling) _____

_____

5. (pioneer/field) _____

_____

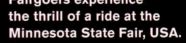

**Fairgoers experience
the thrill of a ride at the
Minnesota State Fair, USA.**

WRITING

ACTIVITY 19 | Following the writing process to write an essay

Step 1: Choose a topic

In this unit, the topic has been chosen for you. Read the assignment.

> *Discuss how the tourist industry has affected Orlando, Florida. Briefly describe the history of the city and tell what events influenced its growth. Explain how the tourist industry has affected the people of Orlando both positively and negatively.*

Step 2: Brainstorm

Read the relevant sources: Paragraph 3.1 "Orlando: From Tiny Town to Major City," Paragraph 3.3 "The Effects of Tourism on One Florida City," and Figure 3.1 "Orlando Sprawl." Highlight the important information in each source. Ask yourself, "What is the author's purpose for writing this information?" Then decide which pieces of information support what the author intended. Group together the ideas that are connected and that support each other.

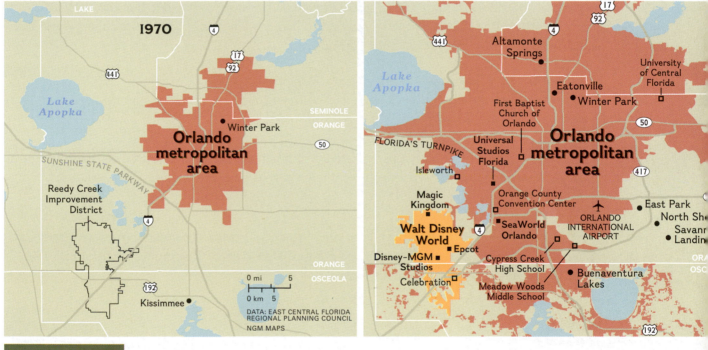

FIGURE 3.1

Orlando Sprawl After Disney World opened in 1971, "Orlando" became the brand name for the sprawl that is central Florida. America's population is decentralizing faster than at any time in history, and Orlando reflects this trend. In three decades, the metropolitan area has grown fivefold in size. Growth is fastest at the city's margins, where the exurbs lure residents with larger houses, new big-box stores, and jobs in the suburbs rather than the city (Allman, 2007).

Allman, T.D. (Mar. 2007). "The themeparking, megachurching, franchising, exurbing, McMansioning of America: How Walt Disney changed everything." *National Geographic Magazine*, pp. 96–116.

Downtown Orlando, Florida, skyline reflected in Lake Eola

Step 3: Outline
On a separate piece of paper, write an outline to help you create a more detailed plan for your essay. Use your ideas from Step 2. Then exchange outlines with a partner. Use the Peer Editing Form 1 for Outlines in the *Writer's Handbook* to help you comment on your partner's work. Use your partner's feedback to revise your outline.

Step 4: Write the first draft
Use your outline and the feedback you received to write the first draft of your essay.

Step 5: Get feedback from a peer
Exchange your first draft with a partner. Read your partner's essay. Then use Peer Editing Form 3 in the *Writer's Handbook* to help you comment on your partner's writing.

Step 6: Reread, rethink, rewrite
Use the feedback to identify three places where you could make revisions to improve your essay. Then write as many drafts as necessary to produce a good essay. Remember to proofread your essay before you submit it to find any errors.

Step 7: Write the final draft

WRITER'S NOTE Proofreading

When you proofread a paper, be sure you are in a place where you can concentrate. This means getting rid of disruptions like cell phones or the TV. If you write on a computer, print a copy of your writing since we read differently on screen and on paper. Read the paper aloud as you may hear errors that your eyes miss. Always check your spelling and punctuation.

Additional Topics for Writing

Here are five more ideas for topics for essay writing. Your teacher may require you to consult one or more sources.

TOPIC 1: Look at the photo on this page. Discuss the origin of two to three popular foods.

TOPIC 2: What are some of the causes of cheating on exams?

TOPIC 3: Explain how a person can quit a bad habit.

TOPIC 4: What are the major differences between a debit card and a credit card? Does one offer more advantages than the other?

TOPIC 5: Should passengers on airplanes be allowed to use their cell phones?

TEST PREP

Write a summary paragraph on the following topic. You should spend about 40 minutes on this task.

Write a summary of one of the essays in Units 1 or 2.

Remember to double-space your essay. Write at least 300 words.

> **TIP**
> Give yourself a few minutes before the end of the test to review your writing. Check for spelling, verb tense, and subject-verb agreement mistakes.

Coffee beans being harvested in Ethiopia. Coffee beans are an important export product for many countries.

4 | Cause-Effect Essays

OBJECTIVES
- Review the structure of a cause-effect essay
- Use transitions in cause-effect writing
- Use verb tenses consistently
- Recognize and avoid sentence fragments
- Write a cause-effect essay

Raccoons gather in New York City's Central Park, hoping for handouts. Feeding these mammals is illegal, and it can also be dangerous as they often carry disease.

FREEWRITE | Look at the photo and read the caption. On a separate piece of paper, write about what kinds of things happen when humans and wild animals share the same space or live too close together.

ELEMENTS OF GREAT WRITING

What Is a Cause-Effect Essay?

A **cause-effect essay** tells how one event (a cause) leads to another event (an effect). A cause-effect essay can:

- analyze the ways in which one or more *effects* result from a particular *cause* (focus-on-effects method);
- analyze the ways in which one or more *causes* lead to a particular *effect* (focus-on-causes method).

In other words, a cause-effect essay may focus on the effects of an issue or on the causes of that issue. Either approach provides a useful means for discussing the possible relationship between the two events.

In cause-effect essays, writers sometimes suggest that because one event preceded another event, the former event caused the latter. However, actions are not necessarily related simply because one follows the other sequentially. You need to be sure that the causes and effects they describe are logically connected.

Organizing a Cause-Effect Essay

There are two main ways to organize a cause-effect essay: **focus-on-effects** or **focus-on-causes**.

A **focus-on-effects essay** on global warming could discuss the many ways that global warming is negatively impacting the habitat of polar bears. The number of paragraphs could vary depending on the number of effects being discussed. If the writer includes three effects, the essay might include five paragraphs and look like this:

INTRODUCTION	Paragraph 1	Hook Connecting information Thesis statement
BODY	Paragraph 2	Effect 1: dangerous swimming conditions • sea-ice platforms farther apart
	Paragraph 3	Effect 2: scarcity of food • fewer hunting opportunities
	Paragraph 4	Effect 3: reduced population • females with less body weight have lower reproduction rates
CONCLUSION	Paragraph 5	Restated thesis Suggestion, opinion, prediction

A **focus-on-causes essay** could discuss the causes of global warming, such as burning fossil fuels and deforestation. The number of paragraphs could vary depending on the number of causes being discussed. If the writer chooses to discuss three causes, then the organization for this essay could have five paragraphs and look like this:

INTRODUCTION	Paragraph 1	Hook Connecting information Thesis statement
BODY	Paragraph 2	Cause 1: human activities • carbon dioxide from vehicles • not recycling (requires creating more products from scratch)
	Paragraph 3	Cause 2: increased industrial activity • greater carbon dioxide from burning fuels to run factories
	Paragraph 4	Cause 3: deforestation • Increased human population requires more space, so trees are cut down. • Fewer trees mean less oxygen, which causes a higher percentage of carbon dioxide in the atmosphere.
CONCLUSION	Paragraph 5	Restated thesis Suggestion, opinion, prediction

Topics for Cause-Effect Essays

What is an appropriate topic for a cause-effect essay? Most writers answer this question by thinking of the final effect or result. The brainstorming stage then requires thinking about one or more causes of that effect.

When selecting topics for this type of essay, a writer should consider relevant questions such as:

- What is the end effect?
- Is there one main effect, or are there several effects?
- Is there one main cause, or are there several causes?

A female polar bear with her cub travel over the sea ice near the arctic village of Barrow, Alaska.

Here are some general topics that lend themselves to a cause-effect essay. Notice that the last two in each group do not use the words *cause* or *effect*.

Topics for Focus-on-Causes Essays	Topics for Focus-on-Effects Essays
The causes of the high divorce rate in some countries	The effects of pollution in my country
The causes of World War I	The effects of high salaries for athletes
The causes of low voter participation in elections	The effects of social media on business
The reasons new teachers quit	The impact of technology on education
Why only a small percentage of people read newspapers today	What happens when a large percentage of adults cannot read well

ACTIVITY 1 | Identifying topics for cause-effect essays

Check the four topics that are appropriate for cause-effect essays. Discuss with a partner why the other topics are not appropriate. Then add two more topics that you think would be suitable for a cause-effect essay.

1. _____ the reasons that Earth's weather has changed so much in the last century

2. _____ Bangkok versus Singapore as a vacation destination

3. _____ a trip to visit my grandparents

4. _____ the increasing use of computers in schools

5. _____ explaining dietary guidelines for children

6. _____ how to play the piano

7. _____ why some students receive scholarships

8. _____ falling birthrates in many countries

9. _____

10. _____

Supporting Details for Cause-Effect Essays

After selecting a topic, you should determine whether to focus more on the causes of the issue or its effects. This process will also help you to select and develop supporting details to strengthen the argument, which is an important step in constructing a solid essay.

When brainstorming an outline, a useful technique is to make two lists. One list should include as many causes as you can think of. The second list should include as many effects or results as you can think of. The list that is bigger should determine the primary focus of your essay.

Here is an example for an essay about the challenge of learning English:

CAUSES OF CHALLENGE	EFFECTS OF CHALLENGE
• English has 14 vowel sounds. • The spelling system is unpredictable. • English has 12 verb tenses. • English has many phrasal verbs and idioms. • English vocabulary comes from many sources including German and Latin.	• Some people study English for years. • People spend a lot of money to learn English. • There are many jobs for teaching English. • Some people have a hard time learning English. • Some people give up studying.

ACTIVITY 2 | Brainstorming for two methods

Imagine you have to write a cause-effect essay about stress. Brainstorm ideas using both the focus-on-effects method and the focus-on-causes method. Discuss your ideas with a partner.

CAUSES OF STRESS	EFFECTS OF STRESS

A student feels the pressure of preparing for the National College Entrance Exam in Anhui Province, China.

ACTIVITY 3 | Studying an example cause-effect essay

Essay 4.1 describes how weather has affected historical events. Discuss the preview questions with a partner. Then read the essay and answer the questions that follow.

1. Can you name a time when the weather affected an event that you attended? Was it a positive effect or a negative effect?

2. In the thirteenth century, a weather event prevented the warrior Kublai Khan from invading Japan by boat. What types of weather do you think could have caused this?

WORDS TO KNOW Essay 4.1

brutal: (adj) hard or uncomfortable
crush: (v) to defeat badly
dense: (adj) crowded together
dreadful: (adj) frightening, terrible
handily: (adv) easily
intervene: (v) to stop an action from happening
overlook: (v) to fail to notice or know about

radically: (adv) completely, thoroughly
reign: (n) the period of time when a king or queen rules
retreat: (v) to go back
span: (v) to extend from one point to another
tempting: (adj) attractive, desirable
unambiguously: (adv) clearly, definitely

ESSAY 4.1 | **APA**

How Weather Has Changed World History

1   It is **tempting** and often comforting to believe that people can control their fate. Of course, the decisions they make daily do affect the course of their lives, but people cannot control every aspect of their lives. Forces beyond their control **intervene** in their affairs. Although many people believe that the weather has little influence in their lives besides determining what clothes they wear on a particular day, the weather has in fact caused world history to **radically** shift in important ways that are still felt today.

2   Numerous examples from world history document the long-term effects of weather in the formation of cultures and nations. In the thirteenth century, Kublai Khan ruled over the vast Mongol Empire, which **spanned** from the Pacific Ocean in the east to the Black Sea in the west, from present-day Siberia in the north to Afghanistan in the south. To expand his **reign** further, Kublai Khan led two invasions of Japan. As a result of two monsoons[1], however, he ended these attacks. Delgado (2008) describes details of this event: "The legend, oft repeated in countless history books, speaks of gigantic ships, numbering into the thousands, crewed by Mongol warriors, and of casualties on a massive scale, with more than 100,000 lives lost in the final invasion attempt of 1281" (p. 4). Because of this unexpected defeat, Kublai Khan decided to stage a third invasion of Japan, but he died before he could fulfill this ambition. Without these monsoons, Japan might have been defeated by the Mongols and thus lost its identity as a unique culture, with far-reaching consequences for Asia and indeed the world today.

[1]monsoon: a heavy rainstorm, especially of Southeast Asia

The Mongols, under Kublai Khan, sought to conquer Japan, but their invading fleet was devastated by storms.

3   Fog played an important role in the outcome of the American Revolution against Great Britain. In the early years of the war, which began in 1775, it appeared very likely that the British would **crush** the armies of her colonial territory and incorporate it back into the empire. The British troops were a well-trained and disciplined army that was feared worldwide. In contrast, the American troops were newly trained, were sometimes poorly organized, and lacked sufficient resources to fight effectively. Commander-in-Chief George Washington could have easily been defeated in the Battle of Long Island on August 22, 1776. Historical records show that Sir William Howe, the British commander, was clearly defeating Washington and was actually winning **handily** (Seymour, 1995). Nonetheless, the weather intervened when a heavy fog rolled in, so the American forces were able to **retreat**, regroup, and survive to fight another day. Due to this fog, the American troops were not defeated in their struggle for freedom. Consequently, today's United Kingdom of England, Wales, Scotland, and Northern Ireland does not include the United States.

4   When Napoleon Bonaparte invaded Russia in the early nineteenth century, he met with early successes that appeared to guarantee that he might eventually rule the world. His soldiers captured Moscow and destroyed the city, which encouraged him to push farther in his military campaigns. However, because his dreams of glory were so strong, Napoleon **overlooked** the simple fact that Russian winters are extremely cold. When the temperatures fell below freezing, many of his soldiers and their horses died in the **brutal** weather. As Belloc (1926) writes in his classic study of the Napoleonic Wars, "The cold *was* the abominable[2] thing: The **dreadful** enemy against which men could not fight and which destroyed them" (p. 217). As a consequence of the failure of Napoleon's Russian campaigns, his own rule ended relatively soon after. His defeat led to a reorganization of power throughout the European nations, as well as the rise of Russia as a major world power.

[2]abominable: disgusting, causing hateful feelings

5   As these three examples **unambiguously** demonstrate, the weather has been a key factor in numerous shifts in world history as well as in power balances among cultures and nations. Without the rainy storms of the monsoon season, Japan might be the eastern outpost of Mongolia; without the appearance of **dense** fog, the United States might still be a territory of the United Kingdom; and without winter snow, Muscovites might speak French. Today weather forecasters can usually predict with a high degree of accuracy when thunderstorms, hurricanes, tsunamis, and tornadoes will strike, but the course of history cannot be fully isolated from the effects of the weather.

References

Belloc, H. (1926). *Napoleon's campaign of 1812 and the retreat from Moscow.* New York: Harper.

Delgado, J. (2008). *Kublai Khan's lost fleet: In search of a legendary armada.* Berkeley, CA: University of California Press.

Seymour, W. (1995). *The price of folly: British blunders in the War of American Independence.* London: Brassey's.

1.   What is the purpose of the essay? Begin with *The purpose of this essay is . . .*

_____

_____

2.   Underline the thesis statement in the essay.

The extreme winter weather in Moscow

3. How is this essay organized? Check the method used.

  ☐ focus-on-causes method   ☐ focus-on-effects method

4. Which citation method is used: APA or MLA? _____

5. Complete the diagram with the causes and effects described in Essay 4.1.

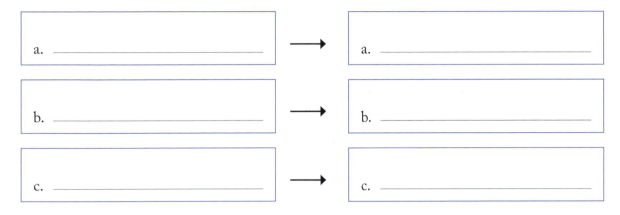

CAUSES

a. _____

b. _____

c. _____

EFFECTS

a. _____

b. _____

c. _____

6. Which details support the thesis statement? What information do you think the writer should have included to make the essay stronger? Discuss with a partner.

ACTIVITY 4 | Completing an Outline

Complete the outline using information from Essay 4.1.

Title: How Weather Has Changed World History

I. Introduction

  A. Hook: Describe _____

  B. Suggest that people cannot control every aspect of their environments.

  C. Thesis statement: _____

II. Body Paragraph 1

  A. Provide the example of Kublai Khan and his invasion of Japan.

  B. Cite the study of J. Delgado, who describes Kublai Khan's failed invasion.

  C. Discuss how _____

III. Body Paragraph 2

    A. Provide the example of _____

    B. Cite the study of W. Seymour, who documents the circumstances of the battle.

    C. Discuss how the United States might have remained a member of the British Commonwealth, if not for a heavy fog.

IV. Body Paragraph 3

    A. Provide the example of Napoleon Bonaparte's invasion of Russia.

    B. Cite the study of _____

    C. Discuss the consequences of Napoleon's defeat in relation to Russia's rise as a world power.

V. Conclusion

    A. Summarize the three examples from the body paragraphs.

    B. Suggest that, although weather forecasters can predict the weather with more accuracy than in the past, _____

_____

Thesis Statements for Cause-Effect Essays

A thesis statement for a cause-effect essay should indicate whether the essay focuses on causes or effects. The thesis statement can use the words *cause(s)* or *effects(s)*, but this is not necessary if the cause or the effect is implied in the thesis. In addition, a thesis statement sometimes includes a number, as in *three causes* or *two effects*. Study these examples:

Focus-on-Causes Thesis Statements

For three important reasons, many customers prefer to shop online.

The increase in obesity in our country is due to food commercials, cheap fast food, and video games.

Focus-on-Effects Thesis Statements

This essay will discuss the effects of watching too much TV on children's family life, interpersonal skills, and school life.

Walking for 20 to 30 minutes per day has several positive effects.

ACTIVITY 5 | Writing thesis statements for cause-effect essays

Write a thesis statement for each topic. Then compare your answers with a partner's.

1. Topic: the effects of cell phone addiction

_____

_____

2. Topic: the effects of being an only child

_____

_____

3. Topic: the reasons for choosing a vegetarian diet

_____

_____

4. Topic: the causes of insomnia

_____

_____

Transitions and Connectors in Cause-Effect Essays

Transitions and connectors can be used to indicate cause or effect relationships. Perhaps the most familiar cause-effect transition is _because_: "X happened **because** Y happened." Here is a list of common transitions for cause-effect essays.

TRANSITIONS AND CONNECTORS	EXAMPLES
TRANSITIONS as a consequence as a result consequently for this reason therefore thus	Industrial activity has increased. **As a consequence,** greenhouse gases have increased.
SUBORDINATING CONJUNCTIONS as because since	**As** industrial activity increases, the amount of greenhouse gases increases.
COORDINATING CONJUNCTIONS so	Industrial activity has increased considerably, **so** greenhouse gases have increased.

TRANSITIONS AND CONNECTORS	EXAMPLES
PREPOSITIONS as a result of because of due to on account of owing to	**Owing to** increased industrial activity, greenhouse gases have increased.
SENTENCE FRAMES a consequence of X is Y an effect of X is Y as a result of X, Y if X … then Y X can lead to Y X is a key factor in Y	Industrial activity is **a key factor in** increased greenhouse gases.

ACTIVITY 6 | Identifying transitions and connectors in an essay

Reread Essay 4.1. Underline eight transitions or connectors that show a cause-effect relationship.

ACTIVITY 7 | Choosing transitions and connectors

Read Essay 4.2 and underline the appropriate transition words or connectors. More than one answer may be possible.

> **WORDS TO KNOW** Essay 4.2
>
> **hypothesis:** (n) an idea or theory that has not been proven
> **justification:** (n) rationale for doing something
> **live within your means:** (phr) to spend only what you can afford
> **obstacle:** (n) something that stops progress
>
> **prospective:** (adj) related to future possibility of happening or coming true
> **reciprocal:** (adj) mutual; referring to an equal exchange
> **seemingly:** (adv) apparently
> **superior:** (adj) of better quality

ESSAY 4.2 **APA**

Causes of Happiness

What makes a person happy? [1](If / So) people want to be happy, should they seek money and professional success? Many experts in fields such as sociology, psychology, and public policy are attempting to answer this **seemingly** simple question of what makes people happy and how communities, social organizations, and employers can facilitate happiness by implementing a few specific strategies. In this new field of happiness studies, some intriguing answers are beginning to emerge about what makes people happy. Surprisingly, they support the longstanding **hypothesis** that money cannot buy happiness.

One of the chief **obstacles** to happiness is referred to as "social comparison". When people compare themselves to other people, they prefer to see themselves as in some way **superior**. In an experiment, social scientists asked whether people would prefer earning $50,000 per year while their peers earned $25,000 per year, or whether they would prefer earning $100,000 per year while their peers averaged $250,000 per year. Even though people would earn more in the latter scenario, most chose the former [2](as a consequence of / because of) their desire to see themselves as more successful than others (Layard, 2005). [3](Owing to / Thus), a simple way to increase happiness is for people to reject the urge to compare themselves to others based on their finances and to **live within their means**.

Another way for people to increase their sense of personal happiness is for them to be true to themselves and keep their personal sense of integrity. While this advice may seem obvious, people who respect and follow their authentic desires generally report being happier than people who do not. As Martin (2012) explains, "At its core, authenticity implies discovering and pursuing what we care about most deeply." He further explains the **reciprocal** relationship between happiness and authenticity: "As much as authenticity contributes to the pursuit of happiness, then, happiness in turn contributes to identifying our authentic selves" (p. 55). When people limit their personal desires [4](in order to / in spite of) obtain certain goals, they may reach those goals but actually end up unhappier.

[5](Finally / Consequently), sometimes people benefit from social rules that encourage them to improve their lives, even when these laws cost more money. While few people enjoy paying taxes, some taxes make people happier [6](although / because) they improve the overall quality of people's lives. In their study of smoking and cigarette taxes, Gruber and Mullainathan (2006) conclude that "taxes may affect the happiness of former smokers (by making it easier to resist the temptation to resume smoking) or **prospective** smokers (by making it easier to never start smoking in the first place)" (p. 139). This example demonstrates how a society's rules [7](are a result of / can lead to) people's happiness, even through the apparently negative practice of increased taxation. Taxes also contribute to the funds available for other social purposes, which is further **justification** for their use.

These are merely three ways that scholars of happiness have determined that people can enhance their personal happiness. People should avoid comparing themselves to others financially. They should seek to live as their authentic selves in their personal and professional lives. [8](Furthermore / Since), they should welcome rules, laws, and even taxes that increase the general happiness of the population. Everyone says they want to be happy, and happiness studies are helping people learn how to lead happier lives rather than to passively expect happiness to find them.

References

Gruber, J., & Mullainathan, S. (2006). Do cigarette taxes make smokers happier? In Ng, Y-K. & Ho, L.S.(Eds.), *Happiness and public policy: Theory, case studies, and implications* (109–146). Basingstoke, England: Palgrave Macmillan.

Layard, R. (2005). *Happiness: Lessons from a new science.* New York: Penguin.

Martin, M. (2012). *Happiness and the good life.* Oxford: Oxford University Press.

Grammar: Consistent Verb Tense Usage

English has 12 verb tenses, but the two most commonly used in academic writing are simple present and simple past tense. An essay may have some information about the past and some information about the present, but most of the information will be about one time period. It is important not to change verb tenses in your writing without a reason for doing so.

EXPLANATION	EXAMPLES
When describing an event in the past tense, maintain the past tense throughout your explanation.	In our experiment, we **placed** three live freshwater plants into a quart jar that **was filled** with fresh water at 70 degrees Fahrenheit. We then carefully **added** a medium-sized goldfish.
When talking about facts that are always true, use present tense.	The sun **is** the center of the solar system. Earth and other planets **revolve** around the sun. Most of the planets **have** at least one moon that **circles** the planet, and these moons **vary** tremendously in size, just as the planets **do**.
In a report, it is possible to have different verb tenses reflecting different times.	According to this report, the police now **believe** that two men **stole** the truck and the money in it.

ACTIVITY 8 | Working with consistent verb tense usage

Read Paragraph 4.1 and correct six verbs where the tense shifts incorrectly.

> **WORDS TO KNOW** Paragraph 4.1
>
> **emit:** (v) to send out, let out   **multiple:** (adj) many, numerous
> **indirect:** (adj) subtle, not definite

PARAGRAPH 4.1

A Simple Experiment

In our experiment, we placed three live freshwater plants into a quart jar that ^was is filled with fresh water at 70 degrees Fahrenheit. We then carefully added a medium-sized goldfish. Next, we tighten the lid and wrapped tape tightly around the lid. This very last step is done to ensure that no air can enter or exit the bottle. The jar was placed on a shelf where it is exposed to **indirect** sunlight for approximately eight hours each day. At one o'clock every day for a week, we observed the fish swimming in the jar. On several occasions, we notice that the plants **emitted multiple** bubbles of a gas. The fish survived for the entire week even though no food or air was provided. Our original hypothesis was that the green plants produced a gas. We now believed this gas was oxygen.

Grammar: Sentence Fragments

Writing a fragment instead of a complete sentence is considered a significant error because it shows a lack of understanding of the basic components of a sentence, namely a subject and a verb that express a complete thought.

TYPE OF ERROR	EXAMPLES
Unattached dependent clause	✗ The average score on the quiz was 97. Because the students had read and studied the textbook. ✓ The average score on the quiz was 97 **because** the students had read and studied the textbook.
No main verb	✗ An essay beginning with a great hook. ✓ An essay beginning with a strong hook **attracts** the reader's attention.
No subject	✗ Is important for children to learn a foreign language. ✓ **It** is important for children to learn a foreign language.

ACTIVITY 9 | Working with fragments

Write *C* if the sentence is complete. Write *F* if the sentence is incomplete. Underline the fragment and correct the error.

_____ **1.** Despite the heavy wind and the torrential rain, the young trees around the lake were able to survive the bad weather. It was a miracle.

_____ **2.** With no remarkable difference except the color of the exterior paint.

_____ **3.** A history of many intriguing stories of leprechauns, fairies, and elves.

_____ **4.** Shopping malls are a popular tourist attraction, but some tourists are not interested in them. Shopping is not that important for everyone.

_____ **5.** Because of the unprecedented popularity of this particular film. Producers were extremely eager to begin work on its sequel.

_____ **6.** Unfortunately, the chef used too much spice in the dishes. The result was that less than half of the food was consumed.

_____ **7.** In the movie, when the two brothers finally meet, the atmosphere is tense. After nearly three decades of separation.

_____ **8.** My mother is so organized that she uses a color-coding system in her kitchen pantry. My father, on the other hand, is completely disorganized.

_____ **9.** Pay a great deal to talk with a so-called expert who claims to be able to understand what dreams mean.

_____ **10.** Thousands of commuters were once again late for work today. Since the bus workers in the area are continuing their strike over pay.

BUILDING BETTER VOCABULARY

WORDS TO KNOW

brutal (adj)	intervene (v) AW	reciprocal (adj)
crush (v)	justification (n) AW	reign (n) AW
dense (adj) AW	live within your means (phr)	retreat (v)
dreadful (adj)	multiple (adj)	seemingly (adv)
emit (v) AW	obstacle (n)	span (v) AW
handily (adv)	overlook (v)	superior (adj)
hypothesis (n) AW	prospective (adj) AW	tempting (adj) AW
indirect (adj) AW	radically (adv) AW	unambiguously (adv) AW

ACTIVITY 10 | Word associations

Circle the word or phrase that is most closely related to the bold word on the left.

1. emit	release	leave
2. brutal	bad	good
3. handily	easily	mainly
4. obstacle	problem	solution
5. unambiguously	clearly	honestly
6. retreat	give again	go back
7. crush	defeat	slowly learn
8. tempting	confusing	inviting
9. hypothesis	dream	idea
10. superior	better	worse

ACTIVITY 11 | Collocations

Fill in the blank with the word that most naturally completes the phrase.

hypothesis	overlook	radically	reciprocal	reign

1. during the king's _____

2. completely _____ the obvious

3. a(n) _____ different idea

4. according to the original _____

5. a(n) _____ agreement

dreadful	multiple	obstacle	retreat	span

6. a serious _____ to achieving a goal

7. the soldiers were ordered to _____

8. _____ several decades

9. a(n) _____ mistake

10. occur _____ times

ACTIVITY 12 | Word forms

Complete each sentence with the correct word form. Use the correct form of the verbs.

NOUN	VERB	ADJECTIVE	ADVERB	SENTENCES
density		dense	densely	**1.** The Netherlands is a _____ populated country. **2.** The air in the room was _____ with smoke.
intervention	intervene	intervening		**3.** When students get too noisy, a teacher needs to _____. **4.** Some say the only solution to the conflict is military _____.
justification	justify	justified justifiable	justifiably	**5.** The judge was shocked at the defendant's poor _____ for the crime. **6.** Students who are unhappy with a grade can ask the professor to _____ the grade. **7.** Nearly everyone recognized the verdict as a _____ decision.
temptation	tempt	tempting		**8.** You should resist the _____ to check your phone late at night. **9.** The job offer was very _____, but I decided not to accept. **10.** It is wise not to _____ thieves by leaving valuables unattended.

Fog hanging over San Francisco, CA

ACTIVITY 13 | Vocabulary in writing

Choose five words from Words to Know. Write a complete sentence with each word.

1. _____

2. _____

3. _____

4. _____

5. _____

BUILDING BETTER SENTENCES

ACTIVITY 14 | Editing

Each sentence has two errors. Find and correct them.

1. Flights from San Francisco were delayed. Because the fog caused limited visible.

2. Barack Obama became the 44th president of the United States in January 20, 2009, and serve two terms for a total of eight years.

3. The country of Singapore was a part of the Federation of Malaya until 1965, that is when it became the independent country.

4. One of the most famous dessert in Argentina is *dulce de leche*, that is a sugary paste that people eat with ice cream.

5. O. Henry is the pen-name of a well-known American author his short story are considered classics.

ACTIVITY 15 | Combining sentences

Combine the ideas into one sentence. You may change the word forms, but do not change or omit any ideas. There is more than one answer.

1. The country of Switzerland lies in Europe.
The country of Austria lies in Europe.
They lie in the center of Europe.
These countries are beautiful.

_____

_____

2. The verb _get_ has many meanings.
These meanings are different.
The verb _get_ is difficult for people.
These people are learning English.

_____

_____

3. The Beatles were a musical group.
They became famous in the early 1960s.
Their fame was international. (Hint: change _international_ to an adverb.)
They were from the United Kingdom.

_____

_____

The Beatles in 1967

ACTIVITY 16 | Responding to teacher feedback

Read the teacher's comments on this first draft. Then rewrite the paragraph.

PARAGRAPH 4.2

add title

_____

word form   *missing word*
One of the most positive <u>outcome</u> of the invention of the light bulb is <u>that has</u> allowed

people to expand their lives into the dark hours of night. Human productivity increased

word order
<u>after this invention significantly</u> because better lighting enabled people to read, study, work, play,

parallel structure   *fragment*
and <u>socializing</u> into the late hours. <u>In addition, the prevalence of affordable lighting. Allowed</u>

<u>companies to continue to manufacture their products during the night hours.</u> Electric lighting

punctuation   *word form*
also enhanced public <u>safety, because</u> city streets were illuminated without the <u>potentially</u> danger

of gas. Now that electric lights are everywhere, it is almost impossible to imagine a world

without them.

One of Joel Sartore's Photo Ark images illuminates the Empire State Building in New York City to draw attention to a species that is facing extinction.

ACTIVITY 17 | Paraphrasing information

For items 1 and 2, choose the best paraphrase of the original sentence. For items 3 and 4, write a paraphrase of the original sentence.

1. Original: No matter how good drivers might be, they can only fully concentrate on one activity at a time, and to do so, they must eliminate all distractions, including cell phones.

   a. Drivers cannot pay attention to multiple things, so they should not look at their cell phones while driving.
   b. Cell phones cause many accidents each year because drivers are distracted.
   c. Drivers are human, and this means they experience multiple types of driving challenges.

2. Original: Several cities have introduced light-rail networks to their transportation systems, but these systems cannot solve all traffic problems.

   a. Cities should not invest in light-rail networks.
   b. Light-rail networks cannot solve all of a city's traffic problems, but several cities have invested in them.
   c. Some cities now use light rail, but they continue to have traffic issues.

3. Original: While many people assume that granola bars are healthy, they can, in many cases, actually be quite high in sugar.

   _____

   _____

4. Original: The population of Earth has risen from 1 billion people in 1800 to 7.7 billion in 2019, and current trends predict even greater growth in the future.

   _____

   _____

WRITING

ACTIVITY 18 | Writing a cause-effect essay

Follow the steps to write an essay. Use at least two words or phrases from the unit.

Step 1: Choose a topic

Choose a topic for which you can think of two or three causes or effects. Your teacher may assign a topic, or you may choose one from the suggestions below.

Humanities	*History*: The causes of an important historical event such as World War I *Language:* The effects of social media on communication
Sciences	*Geology*: The effects of using fossil fuels *Meteorology*: The causes of hurricanes
Business	*Economics*: The causes of inflation in a developing country
Personal	The effects of your personality when dealing with challenges in life

1. What topic did you choose? _____

2. How well do you know this topic? What is your experience with it? Do you need to do more research on the topic?

_____

Step 2: Brainstorm

1. Complete the chart with a list of possible causes and effects for your topic.

CAUSES	EFFECTS

2. Decide which method you think would be better for your essay. If you have more causes, then you should write a focus-on-causes essay with one effect. If you have more effects, then you should write a focus-on-effects essay with one cause.

Step 3: Outline

On a separate piece of paper, use your ideas from Step 2 to write an outline. Exchange your outline with a partner. Use the Peer Editing Form 1 for Outlines in the *Writer's Handbook* to comment on your partner's work. Use your partner's feedback to revise your outline.

Step 4: Write the first draft

Use your outline and the feedback you received to write the first draft of your cause-effect essay.

Step 5: Get feedback from a peer

Exchange your first draft with a partner. Use Peer Editing Form 4 in the *Writer's Handbook* to help you to comment on your partner's writing.

Step 6: Reread, rethink, rewrite

Use the feedback to identify areas where you can improve your essay. Then write as many drafts as necessary to produce a good essay.

Step 7: Write the final draft

Additional Topics for Writing

Here are five more ideas for a cause-effect essay. Follow your teacher's instructions and choose one or more topics to write about.

TOPIC 1: Choose one type of pollution. What are the causes or effects of this type of pollution on the environment?

TOPIC 2: Why do many people prefer foreign goods?

TOPIC 3: Discuss how people's childhood experiences influence their lives.

TOPIC 4: What are the effects of sudden wealth (such as when a person wins the lottery)?

TOPIC 5: What are the effects of overcrowding in cities?

TEST PREP

You should spend about 40 minutes on this task. Write a short essay on the following topic.

What are the benefits—the positive effects—of a good sense of humor? How does a good sense of humor improve one's physical, social, and emotional well-being?

Remember to double-space your essay. Include a short introduction with a thesis statement, three body paragraphs, and a brief conclusion.

> **TIP**
> A rhetorical question is often used as a hook to start an essay. With rhetorical questions, the writer poses a question, which the remainder of the essay should answer.

5 | Comparison Essays

A resident of Stockholm, skates
to work on Lake Mälaren, Sweden.

FREEWRITE | Look at the photo and read the caption. On a separate piece of paper,
write about how this unusual way to commute compares with how you get
to work or school.

ELEMENTS OF GREAT WRITING

What Is a Comparison Essay?

A **comparison essay** analyzes how two related subjects are similar or different. For example, you might compare Julius Caesar and Alexander the Great for an essay on military leaders. Or, if the general topic is forms of urban transportation, you could compare which is more practical—a car or a bicycle.

The subjects that you compare should have some characteristics in common. These common characteristics must be logical to your readers. For example, an essay could compare the differences between a politician in Britain in 1950 and a military leader in China in the 1700s, but what do readers learn from comparing the lives of these two people? What do they have in common? On the other hand, a comparison essay that addresses the lives of two politicians or two military leaders would have a more unified focus and a stronger thesis because the two subjects would share characteristics.

A comparison essay can:

- say that two subjects are more different than similar;
- say that two subjects are more similar than different;
- show how two subjects share both similarities and differences.

In other words, a comparison essay may focus on comparing, on contrasting, or on both.

Organizing a Comparison Essay

There are two basic ways to organize a comparison essay: **point-by-point method** and **block method**. Both styles include an introduction and a conclusion, but the body paragraphs are organized differently. Of these two organizations, the point-by-point method is more common in academic writing because it is a flexible and adaptable form for essays that address more complex concepts.

In the point-by-point method, one point of comparison provides the topic for each body paragraph. In each paragraph, you discuss both subjects in relation to that one point.

In the block method, you present all of the relevant information about one subject first and then all of the relevant information about the other subject. In this method, you list the information in the same order for each subject, a technique called **parallel structure**. For example, if your points of comparison between a car and bicycle are ease, safety, and cost, they should be listed in the same order in each body paragraph. Maintaining parallel structure in sentences and in paragraphs improves the organization of an essay and makes it easier for the reader to follow.

Look at the ways to organize an essay comparing two modes of transportation, a car and a bicycle, for ease of use, for safety, and for cost:

POINT-BY-POINT METHOD	BLOCK METHOD
Introduction Paragraph Hook Connecting information Thesis statement	**Introduction Paragraph** Hook Connecting information Thesis statement
Body Paragraph 1 Point 1: ease of use — car — bicycle	**Body Paragraph 1** Point 1: ease of use of a car Point 2: safety of a car Point 3: cost of a car
Body Paragraph 2 Point 2: safety — car — bicycle	**Body Paragraph 2** Point 1: ease of use of a bicycle Point 2: safety of a bicycle Point 3: cost of a bicycle
Body Paragraph 3 Point 3: cost — car — bicycle	**Body Paragraph 3** (Optional) Evaluation, recommendation
Body Paragraph 4 (Optional) Evaluation, recommendation	
Conclusion Paragraph Restated thesis Suggestion, opinion, or prediction	**Conclusion Paragraph** Restated thesis Suggestion, opinion, or prediction

In academic essays, it is common to include a body paragraph before the conclusion that evaluates which subject is better or more suitable. So, in the previous example, you may want to include a paragraph in which you evaluate the points of comparison between a car and bicycle. You can also add a paragraph to make a longer recommendation to the reader.

Traffic in Ho Chi Minh City, Vietnam

99

Topics for Comparison Essays

A topic for a comparison essay should address two subjects that are related in some way. You must have a logical reason for making the comparison or contrast. A comparison essay also requires a topic for which you can develop solid points (usually two to four) that compare or contrast the two subjects.

When selecting topics to compare or to contrast, consider relevant questions such as:

- What features do the subjects have in common?
- What features do they *not* have in common?
- Can you develop a thesis by comparing and contrasting their traits?
- Do you have enough information about both topics? If not, your essay will not be balanced.

Here are some general topics that lend themselves to a comparison essay. Note that some of these topics are very broad and would need to be narrowed further.

TOPICS FOR COMPARISON ESSAYS	
a book and the movie based on the book	two professional athletes
a current and former leader in your country	two websites for learning English
child care today and child care a century ago	vegetarian and non-vegetarian diets
courses of study at two different colleges	World War I and World War II
two cities	two team sports

ACTIVITY 1 | Identifying topics for comparison essays

Check the four topics that you think are the most appropriate for a comparison essay. Then write two additional topics.

1. _____ The steps in collecting data for a research study

2. _____ Rio de Janeiro versus Tokyo as a site for the Summer Olympic Games

3. _____ Reproductive processes of mammals and reptiles

4. _____ Societies with small families and societies with large families

5. _____ An analysis of voting trends and results in recent elections in Ecuador

6. _____ The career choice of becoming a teacher or a lawyer

7. _____ Daily life for a student at a university

8. _____ Information about llamas in the Andes Mountains in Peru

9. _____

10. _____

Brainstorming with a Venn Diagram

After selecting the topic and two subjects for comparison, you need to identify the similarities and differences between the two subjects. This process will help you to identify supporting details for the essay.

A useful technique for brainstorming a comparison essay is to complete a Venn diagram illustrating the similarities and differences. A Venn diagram consists of two overlapping ovals that each represents one of the two subjects. The shared area in the middle highlights their similarities. The areas not shared highlight their differences.

Here is a Venn diagram for an essay comparing the two countries of Malaysia and Thailand:

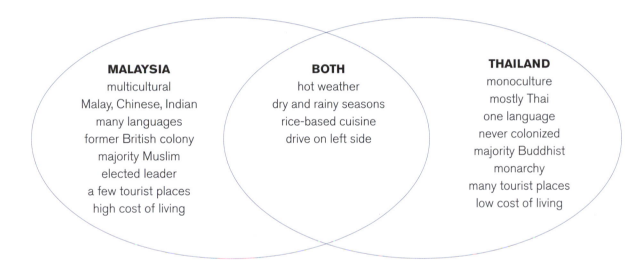

MALAYSIA
multicultural
Malay, Chinese, Indian
many languages
former British colony
majority Muslim
elected leader
a few tourist places
high cost of living

BOTH
hot weather
dry and rainy seasons
rice-based cuisine
drive on left side

THAILAND
monoculture
mostly Thai
one language
never colonized
majority Buddhist
monarchy
many tourist places
low cost of living

A pavilion on a lake near the gardens at Bukit Larut, Malaysia

Twin pagodas built on top of a mountain in northern Thailand

101

ACTIVITY 2 | Brainstorming details for a comparison essay

Select one of the topics you checked in Activity 1. Complete the Venn diagram with similarities and differences between the two subjects. Use your own knowledge or search online.

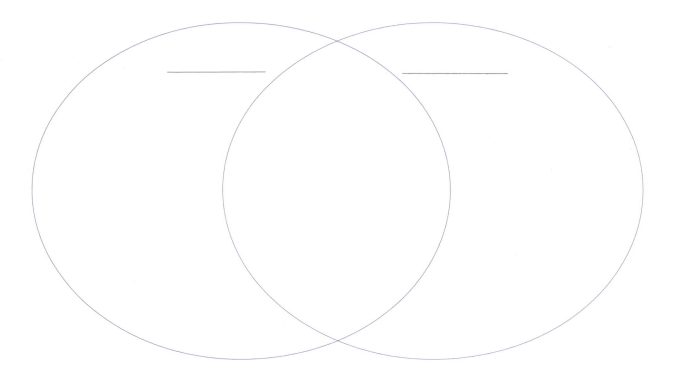

ACTIVITY 3 | Analyzing a comparison essay

Discuss these questions with a partner. Then read Essay 5.1 and answer the questions that follow.

1. Have you, or someone you know, taken an online class? What kind of class was it? Was it a good experience? Explain.

2. Which courses do you think would be best to take online? Which courses would be better to take face-to-face?

WORDS TO KNOW Essay 5.1

address: (v) to discuss; to deal with
allocate: (v) to divide and give something (usually resources) to someone or something
conduct: (v) to perform; to complete
duplicate: (v) to make an exact copy
facilitate: (v) to make easier
isolate: (v) to separate from all others

liability: (n) a drawback; a disadvantage
merge: (v) to blend together to form one
navigate: (v) to move through
prosper: (v) to be successful
reluctance: (n) hesitation to do something
vital: (adj) essential; necessary

Junior high school students using virtual reality simulators in the U.K.

ESSAY 5.1	MLA

Online and Face-to-Face Learning in the Digital Age

1   Would you want to attend school in your pajamas? As computers become increasingly important in education, many schools, colleges, and universities have begun offering online courses and **allocating** resources for the development of online degrees. In this new type of education, some students never set foot on campus to earn a degree. Online learning is causing a revolution in education, but its benefits need to be measured against its **liabilities** when compared to traditional face-to-face instruction. Students should not assume that either online or face-to-face classes are superior; instead, they should focus on what they need to learn from a particular course and which learning paradigm[1] will best **facilitate** their education.

2   Although face-to-face courses are more familiar to many students, online courses offer several advantages. One of the most important of these advantages is that online courses offer greater convenience. In online courses, students may do their coursework according to their own schedules. Because so many of today's students also have work and family responsibilities, it is **vital** that they have the flexibility to fulfill their other obligations while, at the same time, studying. Today many students complete their coursework on weekends or in the middle of the night after they have finished their work and family duties. They no longer have to choose between school and work or between school and family; they can pursue their commitments to both as their schedules allow. Clearly, online courses are more convenient than face-to-face classes.

3   As opposed to some lecture classes, online courses can increase student participation. In large classrooms with 50 or more students, it is often impossible for many students to say anything because the room is so big that not everyone can hear other students well. In addition, some shy students who would hesitate to speak up in a big class may feel

[1]paradigm: an example that serves as a model

more comfortable contributing to class discussions in which they can type their thoughts without having to speak them. In their investigation of online learning strategies, Hiltz and Shea concluded that many online courses "elicit[2] more active participation from students than does the typical face-to-face course **conducted** on the lecture model" (145). Online courses allow students to participate in forums and discussions where they do not feel the pressure of public speaking.

4   Another difference between these two types of education involves the lack of face-to-face communication, which can be a **drawback** to online classes. Despite some students' **reluctance** to speak in class, communicating with others in person is a vital skill for the job market. Students who **isolate** themselves during learning situations may lack the necessary communication skills to succeed in the future. Also, some courses are more difficult to conduct online than in face-to-face settings. For example, courses in foreign languages benefit from classroom environments where students practice speaking to one another. Many science classes require laboratories where students conduct experiments, and drama classes allow students to perform plays. **Duplicating** these experiences online is a challenge for even the best instructors.

5   While face-to-face classes typically do not rely on technology in the classroom, online courses require students to have certain computer skills as well as sufficient technological access to take the courses. Computer usage is widespread, but even today, not all students have their own computers, and many may lack sufficient computer literacy to **navigate** a course's website easily. Under these circumstances, some students may require so much time to find an accessible computer or to learn how to use the course's online tools that they end up with insufficient time and opportunity to complete the coursework. Furthermore, Patel cautions that online courses should "assess the value of technology choices" (9) so that instructors and students can feel confident that these technologies are enhancing the classroom experience, not merely modifying it.

6   Finally, one other way traditional classrooms are different from online classes is that students in online courses do not enjoy as many opportunities to build close, personal relationships with teachers and classmates. In fact, because teachers do not know their students personally, many educators worry about the potential for cheating in online courses. It is quite easy for students to register for an online course and then to hire someone else to take the course for them. Furthermore, many professors hesitate to write recommendation letters for their online students, even those who earn the highest grades in their classes, because they feel uncomfortable advocating for people whom they have never met in person. Teachers of online courses cannot comment on a student's punctuality, presentations in front of others, or interpersonal skills due to the online environment, which does not promote live, human interactions. In this regard, online classes are sometimes not as personal as traditional classes.

[2]elicit: to bring out

7   Both face-to-face and online courses share the same goal of educating students. Since students are drawn to both kinds of courses, it is essential that online courses **address** some of their liabilities and that face-to-face courses take advantage of some of the opportunities available from online learning. Some schools and universities offer mixed-mode courses that combine face-to-face courses with online features. However, mixed-mode courses have their own set of benefits and liabilities. Students need to assess their learning styles, and teachers need to assess their instructional styles, so that both students and teachers can create learning environments where everyone is likely to **prosper**. In the future, these instructional modes could **merge** in interesting ways, and one day, distinctions between online and face-to-face learning may collapse as classrooms are continually reimagined. In such a future, only the best features from these worlds will survive.

Works Cited

Hiltz, Starr Roxanne, and Peter Shea. "The Student in the Online Classroom." *Learning Together Online: Research on Asynchronous Learning Networks,* edited by Starr Roxanne Hiltz and Ricki Goldman, Erlbaum, 2005, pp. 145-68.

Patel, Fay. *Online Learning: An Educational Development Perspective.* Nova, 2014.

1. What is the purpose of this essay? Begin with *The purpose of this essay is . . .*

   _____

   _____

2. What is the writer's thesis statement? Underline it.

3. Is the essay organized by the point-by point method or block method?

   _____

4. What are two advantages of each type of class that the writer discusses?

   Face-to-face: _____

   _____

   Online: _____

   _____

5. Based on the ideas and supporting details in Essay 5.1, which type of class sounds more effective? What information influenced your answer the most?

   _____

   _____

6. Is there any information that the author could have included to make the essay stronger?

   _____

   _____

ACTIVITY 4 | Completing an outline

Complete the outline using information from Essay 5.1.

Title: Online and Face-to-Face Learning in the Digital Age

I. Introduction

   A. Describe increasing importance of computers in education.

   B. Briefly contrast online education with traditional face-to-face classes.

   C. Thesis statement: Students should not assume that either online or face-to-face classes are superior; instead, _____

II. Body Paragraph 1

   A. Discuss convenience of online courses versus face-to-face courses.

   B. Provide example of _____

III. Body Paragraph 2

   A. Discuss _____

   B. Provide scholarly evidence that supports argument that online courses increase student participation.

IV. Body Paragraph 3

   A. Discuss _____

   B. Provide example of specific classroom settings that benefit from face-to-face interaction.

V. Body Paragraph 4

   A. Discuss _____

   B. Suggest that some students spend too much time learning how to use the computer technology rather than concentrating on the subject matter.

VI. Body Paragraph 5

   A. Discuss _____

   B. Provide an example of how teachers cannot write effective recommendation letters for students they do not know personally.

VII. Conclusion

   A. Suggest that students and teachers assess their learning and instructional styles in order to _____

   B. Predict that this issue will be resolved in the future.

Thesis Statements for Comparison Essays

A good thesis statement for a comparison essay indicates whether the essay focuses on similarities, differences, or both. In addition, the thesis statement sometimes uses **hedging words** such as *may, might, can, seem, appear,* or *some.* These words allow you to state your ideas as accurately as possible and avoid overgeneralizations. Another common structure in a thesis for a comparison essay is a connector such as *although, while,* or *despite.*

FOCUS	EXAMPLE THESIS STATEMENTS
Differences	**Although** the end goal of shopping in a store and shopping online is the same, the experiences are very different. **While** Malaysia and Thailand **may seem** similar because they share a common border, they have striking differences.
Similarities	**Despite** obvious differences in the two languages, English and French share a number of important similarities. **While** Nite Owl and Rorschach, the heroes of Alan Moore's *Watchmen,* **appear** to be exact opposites, they share three important qualities that enable their heroic acts.
Both differences and similarities	Both Barbara Ehrenreich's *Nickel and Dimed* and Jeffrey Sachs's *The End of Poverty* propose similar suggestions for ending poverty, yet they approach the topic in different ways.

ACTIVITY 5 | Writing thesis statements for comparison essays

Write a thesis statement for each topic. Compare your statements with a partner's.

1. two popular tourist destinations

_____

_____

2. two professional sports

_____

_____

3. a current leader (or historical person) with a previous leader (or historical person)

_____

_____

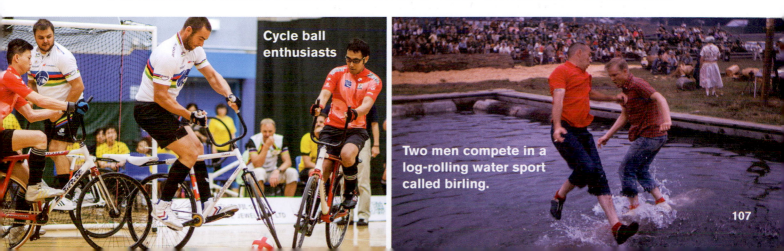

Cycle ball enthusiasts

Two men compete in a log-rolling water sport called birling.

Transitions and Connectors in Comparison Essays

Transitions and connectors help clarify the relationship between the two subjects in a comparison essay. They are especially useful in the point-by-point method in which both subjects are discussed in relation to each point of comparison.

Connectors and Transitions for Similarity and Contrast

SIMILARITY	CONTRAST	EXAMPLES
PREPOSITIONS		
just as like similar to (the same as)	as opposed to contrasted (to / with) different from unlike	**Similar to** rice, potatoes are considered a food staple. **Different from** yogurt, ice cream has a high sugar content.
COORDINATING CONJUNCTIONS		
and . . . too	but yet	Soda is high in sugar, **and** ice cream is **too**. Soda is high in sugar, **yet** it remains popular.
SUBORDINATING CONJUNCTIONS		
	although even though whereas while	Red meat can be high in saturated fats, **whereas** chicken is lower in saturated fats.
TRANSITIONS		
equally in the same way likewise similarly	however conversely on the other hand	Cars require regular maintenance. **Likewise**, bicycles need to be maintained. Cars pollute the air. **On the other hand**, bicycles are environmentally friendly.

ACTIVITY 6 | Identifying transitions and connectors

Find six transitions or connectors in Essay 5.1. Copy them below and write whether they show similarities or differences.

1. Paragraph 2 _____ Shows _____

2. Paragraph 3 _____ Shows _____

3. Paragraph 4 _____ Shows _____

4. Paragraph 5 _____ Shows _____

5. Paragraph 6 _____ Shows _____

6. Paragraph 7 _____ Shows _____

ACTIVITY 7 | Identifying connectors in a comparison essay

Discuss the questions with a partner. Then read Essay 5.2 and choose the words that connect the ideas in the best way.

1. How many zoos have you visited? Which ones and where?

2. Do an Internet search using the phrase "for and against zoos." Read at least two different articles. Tell your classmates what you learned.

WORDS TO KNOW Essay 5.2

ethical: (adj) involving questions about what is right or wrong
extinction: (n) the state of a species no longer existing
habitat: (n) the natural place where a creature lives

hospitable: (adj) having an environment where living things can live or grow easily
indigenous: (adj) native to an area
simulate: (v) to imitate or copy the appearance or characteristic of another thing

---

ESSAY 5.2   **MLA**

Fight for Survival

1   Many mammals—and other animals [1] (both / too)—are facing **extinction**, which threatens the diversity of animal life on Earth. [2] (Unlike / Equally) pets and farm animals, the existence of wild animals such as gorillas and tigers is threatened. To ensure that these creatures are protected and survive in the future, many people believe that they should be in zoos or animal reserves[1]. Zoos keep animals in exhibits where visitors can learn about them, [3] (therefore / whereas) reserves allow animals to move freely in vast expanses of land that better **simulate** their natural living conditions. Both zoos and reserves create **habitats** where animals can reproduce and thus protect their species from extinction, [4] (but / so) both have liabilities as well.

2   Because zoos care for the physical needs of their animals, the animals become tamer[2] than in the wild. For instance, rather than killing their prey themselves, animals are fed by zookeepers. Perhaps the biggest liability of zoos is that they take animals out of their natural habitats and expose them to new climates and conditions, which can present unforeseen dangers and diminish the animals' ability to fend for themselves. Ewen and his colleagues cite several dangers of long-term captivity for animals, including inbreeding, adaptation to captivity, and exposure to non-native parasites[3] (299–308). No matter how

[1]reserve: an area of land for protecting animals
[2]tamer: more domesticated, gentler
[3]parasite: an animal or plant that lives off another

Two lionesses in their natural habitat

hard zoos attempt to simulate natural living conditions, some do not succeed. [5] (Similarly / For example), Kemmerer documents that "sixty percent of zoo-kept elephants suffer from painful and dangerous foot ailments caused by standing on unnatural surfaces" (38). [6] (However / While) trying to protect animals, some zoos harm them instead due to the conditions of the animals' confinement.

3   Animal reserves, [7] (likewise / on the other hand), better resemble the conditions of the wild. Animals must hunt and kill their own prey, and the conservationists do not interact with the animals frequently. [8] (Thus / Whereas), the animals in reserves do not become accustomed to or dependent on humans. In fact, most animal reserves are located within the same geographic region as the **indigenous** animals. [9] (As a result / Conversely), the animals do not need to adjust to a new climate, nor do they encounter parasites or predators they cannot defend themselves against.

4   [10] (However / While) reserves may appear to provide a more **hospitable** environment for animals than zoos, zoos better protect animals from their principal, most dangerous predator: humans. Because reserves are so much larger than zoos, it is quite difficult to police their borders. [11] (Also / Consequently), poachers[4] can break into animal reserves and kill the very animals that the reserves are intended to protect. In addition, some animal reserves act as large-scale zoos for tourists, even though these environments are supposedly set aside to protect and preserve animals.

4poacher: a person who kills and takes animals illegally

5   Zoos and reserves attempt to protect animals. However, whether intentionally or not, [12] (both/ either) habitats potentially harm the animals they seek to protect. Zoos are not as open as reserves, but reserves are not as monitored as zoos. To ensure that future generations of animals escape extinction, the answer might be neither zoos nor animal reserves but simply for humans to leave animals alone in their natural habitat. At the very least, we must find an **ethical** and humane way to preserve all species.

Works Cited

Ewen, John, Doug Armstrong, Kevin Parker, and Philip Seddon. *Reintroduction Biology: Integrating Science and Management.* Wiley-Blackwell, 2012.

Kemmerer, Lisa. "Nooz: Ending Zoo Exploitation." *Metamorphosis of the Zoo,* edited by Ralph Acampora, Lexington, 2010, pp. 37-56.

Grammar: *as . . . as; not as . . . as*

We use *as* + adjective + *as* or *as* + adverb + *as* to show that two things are similar.

> Sudan is **as large as** Algeria.

> Animals in reserves move **as freely as** those in the wild.

In academic writing, we commonly use the negative form of the structure. Note that this is similar in meaning to *less than*.

> This year's winter storm was **not as powerful as** last year's.

> This year's winter storm was **less powerful than** last year's.

ACTIVITY 8 | Writing sentences with *not as . . . as*

Write a true sentence using *not as . . . as* for each topic. Use your own ideas.

1. geography _Egypt is not as large as Saudi Arabia._

2. population _____

3. medicine _____

4. climate _____

5. economy _____

6. history _____

7. education _____

8. personality _____

Grammar: Parallel Structure

Parts of a sentence that have the same function should have the same form—this is called **parallel structure**. Using parallel structure makes your writing easier to understand.

Use parallel structure with lists:

> ✔ In July, the weather is **hot**, **dry**, and very **windy**.
> ✘ In July, the weather is hot, dry, and it is very windy.

Use parallel structure for items in a comparison:

> ✔ **The number of days** in January is greater than **the number of days** in April.
> ✘ The number of days in January is greater than April.

To avoid using the same noun twice, you can use the pronouns *that* (singular) or *those* (plural):

> Good   In some countries, **the cost** of water is higher than **the cost** of oil.
> Better In some countries, **the cost** of water is higher than **that** of oil.

ACTIVITY 9 | Analyzing parallel structure

Find the error in parallel structure in each sentence. Then rewrite the sentence correctly.

1. According to the most recent data, the population of Spain is larger than Greece.

   _____

2. The company's annual report indicates excellent sales in January, March, and in July.

   _____

3. With only five days until the deadline, our team's project is not as good as the other team.

   _____

4. Many children like watching TV shows and to play video games.

   _____

5. To apply for a loan, select from our different loan packages, fill out an application, and you can submit it to a loan officer at the bank.

   _____

6. According to the report, schools in California spend more money per student than New York.

   _____

7. For better heart health, three great forms of exercise involve our legs: jogging, distance running, and when you take fast walks.

   _____

8. To relax, many people like surfing the Internet, working in the garden, and crossword puzzles.

   _____

BUILDING BETTER VOCABULARY

WORDS TO KNOW

address (v)
allocate (v) AW
conduct (v) AW
duplicate (v)
ethical (adj) AW
extinction (n)

facilitate (v) AW
habitat (n) AW
hospitable (adj)
indigenous (adj) AW
isolate (v) AW
liability (n)

merge (v) AW
navigate (v)
prosper (v)
reluctance (n) AW
simulate (v) AW
vital (adj)

ACTIVITY 10 | Word associations

Circle the word that is most closely related to the word on the left.

1. vital	necessary	optional
2. indigenous	native	foreign
3. encounter	find	permit
4. merge	combine	delay
5. simulate	different	similar
6. duplicate	copy	grow
7. reluctance	confusion	hesitation
8. navigate	decide	understand
9. prosper	mention	succeed
10. isolate	alone	allow

ACTIVITY 11 | Collocations

Fill in the blank with the word that most naturally completes the phrase.

extinction	facilitate	habitat	navigate	vital

1. _____ student learning

2. _____ the web site easily

3. the mass _____ of dinosaurs

4. effective planning is _____

5. an animal's natural _____

address	allocate	duplicate	hospitable	reluctance

6. _____ the results of an experiment

7. _____ a problem

8. a(n) _____ environment

9. a(n) _____ to participate

10. _____ enough time for a meeting

ACTIVITY 12 | Word forms

Complete each sentence with the correct word form. Use the correct form of the verbs.

NOUN	VERB	ADJECTIVE	ADVERB	SENTENCES
extinction		extinct		**1.** What caused the mass _____ of the dinosaurs? **2.** What are the effects when an endangered animal becomes _____?
isolation	isolate	isolated		**3.** Being _____ can sometimes make people feel depressed. **4.** Scientists are _____—and then changing—genes that cause diseases.
navigation	navigate	navigable		**5.** The seas around the Cape of Good Hope did not use to be _____. **6.** The college application process is hard to _____.
prosperity	prosper	prosperous	prosperously	**7.** After years of _____, most citizens are happy and content. **8.** The _____ parts of the country are in the northeast.
simulation	simulate	simulated		**9.** A role-play is a _____ of a particular situation. **10.** Before going to space, astronauts _____ working in zero gravity.

The natural habitat for sloths is the rainforests of Central and South America.

ACTIVITY 13 | Vocabulary in writing

Choose five words from Words to Know. Write a complete sentence with each word.

1. _____

2. _____

3. _____

4. _____

5. _____

BUILDING BETTER SENTENCES

ACTIVITY 14 | Editing

Each sentence has two errors. Find and correct them.

1. Before you start write a paragraph or an essay, you should make simple outline.

2. Giraffes eat only leaves, so they live usually in areas with lot of green vegetation.

3. Miami may have more people than any another city in Florida, but the capital city has been Tallahassee.

4. Three great gift ideas for a recent college graduate includes the cash, clothing, and travel.

5. The article indicates how many adult have to wear glasses or contacts for read well.

ACTIVITY 15 | Combining sentences

Combine the ideas into one sentence. You may change the word forms, but do not change or omit any ideas. There is more than one answer.

1. Some people wake up very early.
   They do this every day.
   They do this in order to have some quiet time before the rest of their family wakes up.
   They do this in order to get to their office early.

   _____

   _____

2. A Boeing 737 jet seats 140 passengers.
   140 is an approximate number.
   A Boeing 737 is one of the most common commercial planes.

   _____

   _____

3. The top three names for baby girls in England are Sophia, Olivia, and Emma.
   The next two names on that list are Isabella and Ava.
   This was according to a credible website.

   _____

   _____

ACTIVITY 16 | Paraphrasing

For items 1 and 2, choose the best paraphrase of the sentence. For 3 and 4, write a paraphrase of the original sentence.

1. Because so many of today's students have work and family responsibilities beyond their coursework, it is vital that they have flexibility to fulfill their other obligations while also tending to their studies.

   a. Today so many students have work and family to take care of in addition to their schoolwork, but it is important they have the flexibility to complete everything in their personal life and studies.

   b. Students today work so much that their schedules are more complicated than at any point in history.

   c. Students today are busy both in and out of the classroom, so they need time to meet personal and academic responsibilities.

2. Although dark green vegetables such as spinach and broccoli are loaded with important nutrients, few people actually like to eat these foods.

   a. It is unfortunate that most people do not like to eat dark green vegetables like spinach and broccoli because they are good for our health.

   b. Spinach and broccoli are good for our health.

   c. There are many kinds of dark green vegetables that are good for our health, but most people only know about spinach and broccoli.

3. To ensure that future generations of animals escape extinction, the answer might be neither zoos nor animal reserves but simply for humans to leave animals alone in their natural habitat.

Paraphrase: _____

_____

4. Finally, one very important difference between traditional and online classes is that students in online courses do not enjoy as many opportunities to build personal relationships with teachers and classmates throughout their education.

Paraphrase: _____

_____

_____

WRITING

ACTIVITY 17 | Writing a comparison essay

Follow the steps in the writing process to write a comparison essay.

Step 1: Choose a topic

Choose a topic for a comparison essay. Your teacher may assign a topic, you may think of one yourself, or you may choose one from the suggestions in the chart below.

HUMANITIES	*Literature*: Compare two authors. *History*: Compare two leaders. *Psychology*: Compare two kinds of personalities.
SCIENCES	*Biology*: Compare two diseases. *Astronomy*: Compare two planets.
BUSINESS	*Consumer affairs*: Compare two stores that sell similar products. *Marketing*: Compare two kinds of advertising.
PERSONAL	Compare two important days in your life. Why was each day so important?

1. What topic did you choose?

_____

2. How well do you know this topic? What is your experience with it? Do you need to do more research on the topic?

_____

Step 2: Brainstorm

1. Complete the Venn diagram with similarities and differences between the two subjects you are comparing.

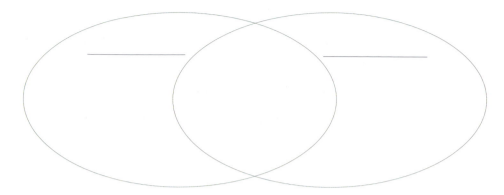

2. Decide if you are going to focus on the similarities or the differences between the two subjects or on both similarities and differences. Then choose three points of comparison that you will use and list them here.

_____

_____

_____

Step 3: Outline

On a separate piece of paper, write an outline to help you create a more detailed plan for your essay. Use the point-by-point method or block method for organizing your essay. Use your ideas from Step 2. Then exchange your outline with a partner. Use the Peer Editing Form 1 for Outlines in the *Writer's Handbook* to help you comment on your partner's work. Use your partner's feedback to revise your outline.

Step 4: Write the first draft

Use your outline and the feedback received to write the first draft of your comparison essay.

Step 5: Get feedback from a peer

Exchange your first draft with a partner. Read your partner's first draft. Then use Peer Editing Form 5 in the *Writer's Handbook* to help you to comment on your partner's writing.

Step 6: Reread, rethink, rewrite

Revise your first draft. Use the comments from your partner to help you edit and revise your writing. Be sure that you use correct vocabulary, correct punctuation, and clear language. Write as many drafts as necessary to produce a good essay. Remember to proofread your essay several times before you submit it so that you find all the mistakes and correct them.

Step 7: Write the final draft

Additional Topics for Writing

Here are five more topics for a comparison essay. Follow your teacher's instructions and choose one or more topics to write about.

TOPIC 1: Compare and contrast two popular travel destinations.

TOPIC 2: Choose a large city and a small or an average-sized city that you know. Which one offers a higher quality of living? Why?

TOPIC 3: Compare and/or contrast two local restaurants.

TOPIC 4: Which provides a better living situation, a house or an apartment? Why?

TOPIC 5: Compare and/or contrast two extreme sports.

TEST PREP

Write a comparison essay on the following topic. You should spend about 40 minutes on this task.

> *Compare watching a movie at home and watching a movie in a theater.*

For this assignment, use the point-by-point method. Remember to double-space your essay. Include a short introduction with a thesis statement, three body paragraphs, and a brief conclusion.

TIP

On some tests, you need to compare and contrast two pieces of information about a topic. For example, you might be asked to read a short passage and then listen to a short recording on the same topic. The strategies for comparing these successfully are the same: take good notes, make a Venn diagram, and see what is similar and what is different.

Young men practice *power-bokking*, an extreme sport in which players are thrown into the air by gear strapped to their legs in Prague, Czech Republic.

6 | Reaction Essays

The Zenith Building in Busan, South Korea, is the highest residential building in Asia. The curvilinear forms were designed to take advantage of views and daylight, as well as to minimize the effects of wind forces.

FREEWRITE | Look at the photo and read the caption. What is your reaction to this photo? What interests or surprises you about the photo? Write your ideas on a separate piece of paper.

ELEMENTS OF GREAT WRITING

What Is a Reaction Essay?

In **reaction essays,** writers share their personal response to a subject. Virtually anything you see or hear could be the subject of a reaction essay—from books, movies, and video games to news reports, information graphics, and scientific studies. The inspiration for a reaction essay is referred to as a **prompt.** Common types of reaction writing include reviews, editorials, and blog journals.

A reaction essay includes—but is not limited to—your opinion about the prompt. Because a reader might be unfamiliar with what you are responding to, you should identify the prompt and summarize its contents well enough so that the reader can understand. The summary should be a key point of a reaction essay, but the thesis statement and your personal response to the prompt are the essay's central focus.

Topics for Reaction Essays

When brainstorming topics for a reaction essay, think of written or visual material—a prompt— you have recently encountered and ask these questions:

1. What is it about this prompt that interests you?

2. How did you respond to the prompt?

3. Why do you want to share your response to the prompt with your readers? What do you want them to learn about it?

4. Can you expand on your reaction to it (rather than simply saying that it is "good" or "bad")?

Here are some general topics and prompts that lend themselves to a reaction essay:

General Topics for Reaction Essays	
A favorite—or least favorite—movie	A surprisingly good book
An interesting blog that you read frequently	An article with which you agree or disagree
An intriguing news report	A piece of art such as a painting or photo

ACTIVITY 1 | Identifying prompts for reaction essays

Check (✓) the four prompts for a reaction essay that interest you the most and that you could most easily respond to.

_____ **1.** An article about the most dangerous animals and insects in Australia

_____ **2.** An announcement on a college's new scholarship policy

_____ **3.** A travel magazine's list of the top 10 things to do in your town/city

_____ **4.** A pie chart showing the number of speakers of the top world languages

Machu Picchu, Peru

_____ **5.** A famous painting

_____ **6.** An article on why so many teachers quit after just a few years

_____ **7.** A graphic showing which kinds of jobs will probably disappear by 2030

_____ **8.** A photo of Machu Picchu in Peru

Organizing a Reaction Essay

Like other essays, a reaction essay requires an introductory paragraph with a thesis, one or more body paragraphs that develop the thesis, and a conclusion that summarizes the response. There are several ways to organize a reaction essay, but one simple pattern includes four paragraphs: an introduction, two body paragraphs that describe your reactions, and a conclusion.

The Introduction

The introduction to a reaction essay includes an overview or summary of the prompt and a thesis statement with your response to the prompt. The overview of the prompt should include citation information. For example, in a reaction essay about an article listing the 10 happiest countries in the world, you should include a sentence that introduces the prompt by name with proper in-text citation:

> In her article "These Are the Top 10 Happiest Countries in the World," Mejia (2018) uses data from the United Nations Sustainable Development Solutions Network to introduce the happiest countries and offer reasons these countries have made this enviable list.

At the end of the essay, you should include a bibliographic entry for this prompt.

Supporting Details

One way to organize a reaction essay is for one of the body paragraphs to discuss parts of the prompt that were as you expected and explain why, while the next body paragraph discusses parts of the prompt that were surprising and explains why. You might consider other emotional reactions to the prompt, such as pleasure, sadness, fear, hope, disappointment, or even anger.

Of course, a reaction essay may be longer than four paragraphs. For some assignments, you can introduce other reactions in additional body paragraphs. These paragraphs could focus on different aspects of the prompt such as:

- a second emotional response that you have
- a different aspect of the prompt (e.g., the reasons the artist painted a painting)
- the style of presentation (e.g., the writing style or the writer's tone)
- the visual impact (e.g., the camera's framing of a movie, the design of a website)

As you plan your essay, consider your personal experiences, your knowledge of the topic, and the reasons behind your response to the prompt. Is your response based on logic and facts, on emotion and feelings, or on both logic and emotion?

Example Organization of a Reaction Essay

In a reaction essay, writers need to be specific about which parts of the prompt they are responding to. For example, if you are writing a review of a movie, you could respond to any number of its elements, as outlined here:

Introduction Paragraph

Introduce the name of the movie and summarize the plot. Include a thesis statement that explains your overall reaction.

Body Paragraph 1

Discuss your reaction to the characters. Did they seem real to you? Were they believable?

Body Paragraph 2

Discuss your reaction to the directing. Was it good? Was it poor? Give reasons.

Fig. 6.1 Lost and Tossed

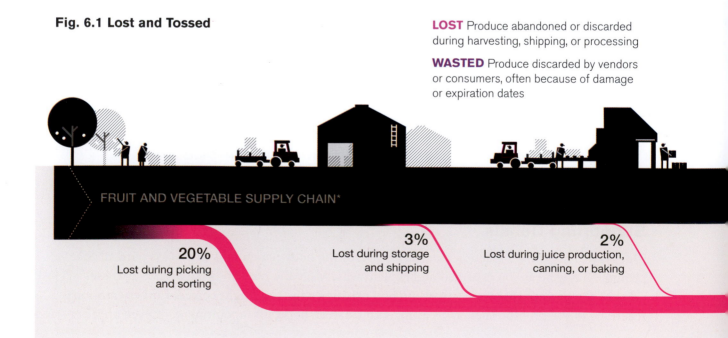

LOST Produce abandoned or discarded during harvesting, shipping, or processing

WASTED Produce discarded by vendors or consumers, often because of damage or expiration dates

FRUIT AND VEGETABLE SUPPLY CHAIN*

20% Lost during picking and sorting

3% Lost during storage and shipping

2% Lost during juice production, canning, or baking

Body Paragraphs 3+

If there are more aspects of the movie that you would like to react to, you can add paragraphs. For example, you could comment on the dialogue—was it natural? If the movie was set in the 1800s, did the language sound appropriate for that era? Give details to support your ideas.

Concluding Paragraph

Summarize your reaction. Include a statement that puts forth a final opinion about the creation or the creator, or a prediction about anything related to this creation or creator.

WRITER'S NOTE Planning the Number of Paragraphs Needed

In some writing classes, the instructor may ask for a five-paragraph essay. However, an essay can have as few as three paragraphs and as many as ten (or more) paragraphs, as long as there is a clear beginning, a body, and a conclusion. The content of the essay, not the type of writing, determines the number of paragraphs that a particular essay has.

ACTIVITY 2 | Brainstorming details for a reaction essay

What are your reactions to Figure 6.1? Write two things about the graphic and content that are as you would expect and two things that surprise you.

As you expected:

1. _____

2. _____

Surprises:

1. _____

2. _____

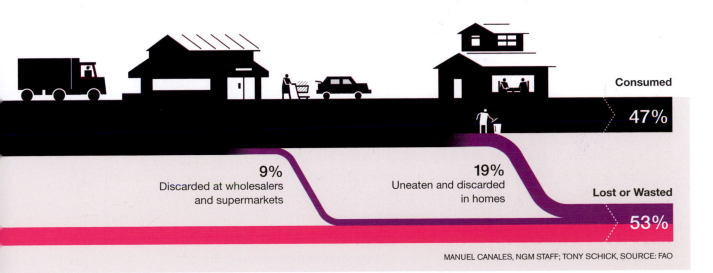

MANUEL CANALES, NGM STAFF; TONY SCHICK, SOURCE: FAO

ACTIVITY 3 | Analyzing a reaction essay

Discuss these questions with a partner. Then read Essay 6.1 and answer the questions that follow.

1. How much food do you waste each week? Examples include not eating everything on your plate at a meal or throwing away food that is spoiled.

2. Is there one food item or food category that you think you waste more than others?

WORDS TO KNOW Essay 6.1

alarming: (adj) signaling danger
commodity: (n) a product for sale, like grains and metals
depict: (v) to illustrate, show
disturbing: (adj) upsetting, unsettling
edible: (adj) can be eaten

expire: (v) (for food) to no longer be good or safe to eat
readily: (adv) easily, without difficulty
revelation: (n) a surprising disclosure
staggering: (adj) overwhelming
taken aback: (adj phr) shocked, surprised

ESSAY 6.1   **APA**

The Shocking Truth about Food Waste

1   Food is one of our most precious **commodities**, so who would imagine that so much of the world's food is actually thrown away each year? The National Geographic graphic "Lost and Tossed" (2016) **depicts** in a clear and comprehensible way the **staggering** amount of **edible** food that is wasted each year. Given that, globally, so many people suffer from serious hunger, the information presented in this visual is especially **alarming**.

2   The most distressing **revelation** in the graphic is that more fruits and vegetables are lost or wasted (53 percent) than actually eaten (47 percent). The graphic shows that this loss and waste happen throughout the production process—from picking food on the farm to throwing out food at home. Furthermore, along with another study (Conrad, Niles, Neher, Roy, Tichenor, & Jahns, 2018) suggesting that "the average person living in America wastes nearly one pound of food daily" (14), this graphic shows that all of us—from farmers to consumers—need to decrease food waste.

3   With regard to other parts of the graphic, another **disturbing** statistic is that 20 percent of food loss happens during picking and sorting. Even though every production process involves some loss of product, this amount is too high. With modern agricultural equipment and technology **readily** available, how is it possible to waste that much food?

4   Finally, I was **taken aback** by how much food consumers waste. The graphic reveals that nearly 20 percent of fruits and vegetables purchased by consumers is unnecessarily wasted. Without a doubt, this is unacceptable. Consumers have full control when it comes to purchasing food. Why is it considered tolerable to buy food that one later throws out because it **has expired**? This food waste is not only unacceptable, but it is also a slap in the face to the millions of people who are suffering from hunger around the globe.

A refrigerator spilling over with carryout containers makes it hard to keep track of food before it spoils.

Using local vegetables while they are still fresh requires careful meal planning and proper storage.

5   The information in the graphic is shocking and sad. Indeed, just as most people cannot imagine wasting food, they are shocked to find out how much food is actually wasted every day. Some of this wasted food is a normal part of the process. However, much of this food waste happens for preventable reasons—which is precisely why I find this information so sad. With a graphic like this that illustrates the depth of this problem so clearly, I predict we will be more motivated to do our part toward reducing food waste.

References

Canales, M., & Schick, T. (2016). *Lost and tossed: Fruit and vegetables*. National Geographic. Retrieved from http://visualoop.com/infographics/lost-and-tossed-fruit-and-vegetables

Conrad, Z., Niles, M., Neher, D., Roy, E., Tichenor, N., & Jahns, L. (2018). Relationship between food waste, diet quality, and environmental sustainability. PLoS ONE 13, 1-18. https:// doi. org/10.1371/journal.pone.0195405

1. What is the purpose of the essay? Begin with *The purpose of this essay . . .*

    _____

    _____

2. Underline the sentence where the writer summarizes and describes the prompt.

3. What adjective(s) does the writer use to indicate her reaction to the *quality* of the graphic?

    _____

4. What adjective does the writer use to indicate her reaction to the *topic* of the graphic?

_____

5. What is the writer's thesis statement?

_____

_____

6. Which of the writer's details do you think most strongly support the thesis statement?

_____

_____

7. What information do you think the writer could have included to make the essay stronger?

_____

_____

ACTIVITY 4 | Analyzing the organization of an essay

Complete the outline using information from Essay 6.1.

Title: The Shocking Truth about Food Waste

I. Introduction

   A. Briefly mention how precious food is for humanity.

   B. Cite National Geographic's visual of food loss.

   C. Thesis statement: _____

   _____

II. Body Paragraph 1

   A. Most distressing revelation in the graphic: _____

   _____

   B. State that this graphic shows that all of us need to reduce food waste.

III. Body Paragraph 2

   A. Another disturbing statistic about food loss: _____

   _____

   B. Rhetorical question: _____

IV. Body Paragraph 3

   A. Discuss how consumers contribute to food loss—20%.

   B. This waste is unacceptable: it is insulting to _____

V. Conclusion

   A. Prediction: _____

Thesis Statements for Reaction Essays

A thesis statement for a reaction essay indicates your primary response to the prompt. Whether that reaction is surprise, like, dislike, outrage, or any other response, you should clearly indicate the reason for your response.

prompt   reaction   reasons

The **new dietary guidelines** are **better than previous ones** because **they offer clearer suggestions about sugar intake**.

If the primary reaction to the prompt is negative, it is common to include a positive statement before introducing the main response. In this case, connectors like *but, yet, however,* and *although* contrast the positive and negative reactions.

The new dietary guidelines contain some clearer suggestions **but** not enough advice about the optimal amount of carbohydrates in a healthy diet.

Thesis statements—and other sentences in a reaction essay—often include adverbs of emphasis and similar phrases to indicate the depth of your response.

The new dietary guidelines are **significantly** better because they offer clearer suggestions about sugar intake.

Here are some common adverbs of emphasis:

absolutely	clearly	definitely	especially	exceptionally
incredibly	obviously	particularly	positively	significantly

ACTIVITY 5 | Writing thesis statements

Write a thesis statement that best captures your response to each prompt. Use an adverb of emphasis in each.

1. Figure 6.1 (use your notes from Activity 2)

_____

_____

2. A movie that you saw recently

_____

_____

3. Your school's website

_____

_____

Transitions in Reaction Essays

Precise use of transitions helps you properly introduce and explain your reactions to a prompt.

PURPOSE	TRANSITION	EXAMPLE
To refer to part of a prompt	concerning regarding with regard to	**Concerning** the design, the graphic is professionally put together.
To add more information about an idea	additionally furthermore moreover	**Furthermore**, the information in the chart is clear and understandable.
To emphasize the importance of an idea	in fact indeed of course without (a) doubt	**Indeed**, a clear and visually attractive graphic helps people understand complex information.

ACTIVITY 6 | Identifying transitions

Reread Essay 6.1. Underline four sentences that include transition words and phrases from the chart above. Discuss with a partner how these sentences help support the writer's ideas.

Grammar: Adverb Clauses

Adverb clauses are used to show relationships between ideas. Adverb clauses answer the questions *when, how, why,* and *under what condition*. An adverb clause is linked to a main clause by a **subordinating conjunction** (e.g., *because*).

main clause   *adverb clause*

Many people refer to this website **because it reports the news accurately**.

Adverb clauses can appear before or after the main clause, though they often begin sentences in academic writing. Varying the order of adverb clauses enhances the readability of one's writing. Note that a comma is required when the adverb clause begins the sentence.

PURPOSE	SUBORDINATING CONJUNCTION	ADVERB CLAUSE
To show cause and effect	because since	Many people refer to this website **because it reports the news accurately.**
To show a condition	if even if unless	**Even if a treaty is signed tomorrow,** true peace may never come to the region.
To show a contrast	although even though whereas while	The candidate for state governor lost **even though he had the full support of the president.**

	after before since until when whenever	**After the war ended,** reconstruction slowly began.
To indicate time		
To show purpose	in order that so (that)	The entry fee was waived **so that everyone could see the exhibition.**

ACTIVITY 7 | Completing adverb clauses

Complete the sentences with the most appropriate subordinating conjunction. Add a comma if necessary.

before	even if	even though	because	in order that	whereas

1. Long _____ Colgate started selling its toothpaste in the 1800s the ancient Egyptians had a recipe for it.

2. At college, students learn key skills _____ they can be prepared for a good job after graduation.

3. This website is especially useful for young teens _____ it was originally designed for the people of their grandparents' age.

4. _____ the senator's popularity is so low it is unlikely that he will win in the next election.

5. _____ the team wins all its remaining games it will have a losing record for the year.

6. Some sociologists note that the rich are getting richer _____ the poor are getting poorer.

ACTIVITY 8 | Using transitions and subordinating conjunctions

Essay 6.2 describes a writer's reaction to a "best-of" list. Read the essay and add the appropriate transitions or subordinating conjunctions. More than one answer may be possible.

> **WORDS TO KNOW** Essay 6.2
>
> **compile:** (v) to put together item by item
> **eagerly:** (adv) with desire or interest
> **poll:** (n) a survey of opinions among people
>
> **rank:** (v) to have a certain place or position in an ordered group
> **reputable:** (adj) honest; with a good reputation

The Square Djemaa el Fna, Marrakech, Morocco, at sunset

An Amazing Variety of Travel Destinations

1   What links Paris, Marrakech, and Siam Reap? Each year the travel website TripAdvisor **compiles** a list of the top 25 tourist destinations based on results from millions of tourists. Based on the 2018 **poll** ("Top 25 destinations – World," 2018), the top destinations included nine in Asia, seven in Europe, three in North America, two in South America, two in the Middle East, one in Africa, and one in Australia. [1] _____ some of the results of this **eagerly** awaited poll were predictable, a few places struck me as particularly interesting choices.

2   [2] _____ I saw that seven of the top ten destinations were in Europe, I was not surprised. Europe is popular, and many people dream about going to Europe. They know about the Eiffel Tower in Paris or Buckingham Palace in London [3] _____ they have seen these tourist sites in photos. [4] _____, it is likely that they have friends or family who have been there and talked about their trips.

3   [5] _____ some of the other places in the top 25, many came as a complete surprise to me. [6] _____ the Red Sea is an important tourist destination in Egypt, I was surprised to see it on this world list. [7] _____, I would have expected Cairo or Giza with its massive pyramids to be top, not a beach resort. [8] _____, I was surprised to see Jamaica and Playa del Carmen, Mexico, on this list. [9] _____ I like these places, I have seen photos of better beaches such

as Waikiki Beach in Hawaii. Two other places that surprised me were Hanoi and Siam Reap. **10** _____, I am glad to see they made the list because these places have a great deal to offer tourists.

4   Perhaps a fair way to summarize my reaction to TripAdvisor's top 25 list is to say that I was not surprised so much by the top ten but that several cities in the remaining fifteen were not ones that I expected. TripAdvisor is certainly a well-known and **reputable** organization, but I hope that any future lists will include some justification of how the sites were chosen and **ranked**.

References

Top 25 destinations – World. (2018, September 3). Retrieved from https://www.tripadvisor.com/
    TravelersChoice-Destinations-cTop-g1

BUILDING BETTER VOCABULARY

WORDS TO KNOW

alarming (adj)	eagerly (adv)	readily (adv) **AW**
commodity (n) **AW**	edible (adj)	reputable (adj)
compile (v)	expire (v)	revelation (n) **AW**
depict (v) **AW**	poll (n)	staggering (adj)
disturbing (adj)	rank (v)	taken aback (adj phr)

ACTIVITY 9 | Word associations

Circle the word or phrase that is most closely related to the word or phrase on the left.

1.	alarming	shocking	visible
2.	commodity	product	need
3.	compile	organize	teach
4.	depict	find	show
5.	edible	can eat	can read
6.	expire	leave	end
7.	rank	order	travel
8.	reputable	respectable	repeat
9.	revelation	possibility	announcement
10.	taken aback	surprised	returned

ACTIVITY 10 | Collocations

Fill in the blank with the word or phrase that most naturally completes the phrase.

compile	disturbing	eagerly	poll	ranked

1. _____ await a response

2. _____ as the best in the world

3. deeply _____

4. _____ a list

5. a recent opinion _____

alarming	expire	readily	revelation	taken aback

6. a(n) _____ report

7. be _____ by surprising news

8. _____ available

9. due to _____ soon

10. an embarrassing _____

ACTIVITY 11 | Word forms

Complete each sentence with the correct word form. Use the correct form of the verbs.

NOUN	VERB	ADJECTIVE	ADVERB	SENTENCES
disturbance	disturb	disturbing disturbed	disturbingly	1. The bad news _____ supporters of the president. 2. There has been a _____ increase in rates of extreme poverty.
eagerness		eager	eagerly	3. Children are usually _____ to open their birthday gifts. 4. The passengers were _____ waiting to board the plane.
expiration	expire	expired		5. A passport usually _____ after 10 years. 6. She got a ticket because she was driving with an _____ driver's license.

reputation		reputed	reputably	7. The company stands by its
				_____ for service.
				8. This computer is _____ one of the fastest on the market.
revelation	reveal	revealed revealing revelatory		9. This decision _____ the company's flawed thinking.
				10. An embarrassing _____ can ruin a political campaign.

ACTIVITY 12 | Vocabulary in writing

Choose five words from Words to Know. Write a complete sentence with each word.

1. _____

2. _____

3. _____

4. _____

5. _____

BUILDING BETTER SENTENCES

ACTIVITY 13 | Editing

Each sentence has two errors. Find and correct them.

1. Although the United Kingdom and New Zealand are similar for size, but New Zealand has just under 5 million people while the United Kingdom has more than 63 million people.

2. Because of Vietnam has such an incredible variety of interesting places to see and experience, more than 10 millions tourists visit this country each year.

3. One thing that makes Arabic as a foreign language difficult to master is that many different dialects are spoken, which mean that the Arabic in Egypt may not resemble to the Arabic in Morocco or Oman.

4. Few people outside the city of Pittsburgh knows about its riverside trails where people bike or jog and enjoying the river scenery.

5. According a reputable higher education website, at least 38 schools in the United Kingdom that offer courses in chemical engineering at the undergraduate level.

ACTIVITY 14 | Combining sentences

Combine the ideas into one sentence. You may change the word forms, but do not change or omit any ideas. There is more than one answer.

1. At least 20 percent of fruits are lost.
At least 20 percent of vegetables are lost.
This happens during picking.
This also happens during sorting.
This information is alarming.

_____

_____

2. English has verb tenses.
There are 12 verb tenses.
One verb tense in English is the present perfect tense.
The present perfect tense is one of the most difficult verb tenses.
This tense is difficult for English language learners.

_____

_____

3. English is an official language in New Zealand.
Maori is an official language in New Zealand.
Sign language is an official language in New Zealand.
There are three official languages.
Many people are surprised to learn this.

_____

_____

Auckland, New Zealand, is a city of volcanoes and water.

ACTIVITY 15 | Responding to teacher feedback

Read the teacher's comments on this first draft. Then rewrite the paragraph.

PARAGRAPH 6.1

Banning Plastic Straws

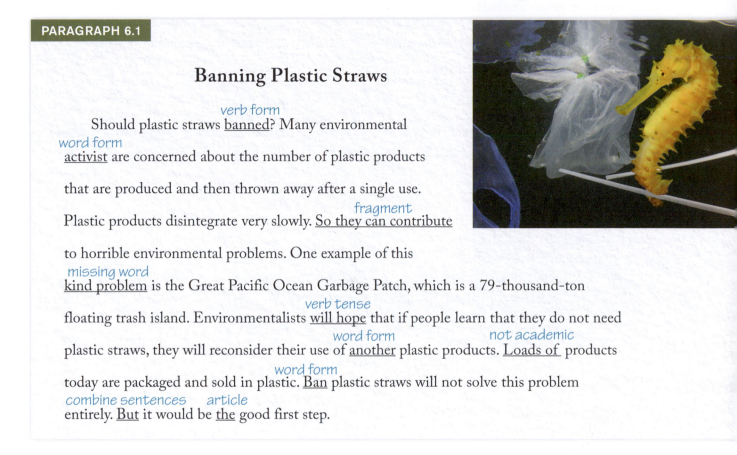

verb form
Should plastic straws <u>banned</u>? Many environmental
word form
<u>activist</u> are concerned about the number of plastic products

that are produced and then thrown away after a single use.
fragment
Plastic products disintegrate very slowly. <u>So they can contribute</u>

to horrible environmental problems. One example of this
missing word
<u>kind problem</u> is the Great Pacific Ocean Garbage Patch, which is a 79-thousand-ton
verb tense
floating trash island. Environmentalists <u>will hope</u> that if people learn that they do not need
word form   *not academic*
plastic straws, they will reconsider their use of <u>another</u> plastic products. <u>Loads of</u> products
word form
today are packaged and sold in plastic. <u>Ban</u> plastic straws will not solve this problem
combine sentences   *article*
entirely. <u>But</u> it would be <u>the</u> good first step.

ACTIVITY 16 | Paraphrasing practice

For items 1 and 2, choose the best paraphrase of the sentence. For 3 and 4, write a paraphrase of
the original sentence.

1. Some economists recommend free trade between nations without any taxes on imports,
    while others believe that regulated trade results in increased prosperity.

    a. Economists do not agree on how much tax should be charged for importing regular
        goods.
    b. Economists disagree about the benefits of controlling trade between countries.
    c. Some economists support free trade without any taxes on imports, but others believe that
        we will prosper more if we regulate it.

2. As costs decrease, virtual reality headsets are becoming increasingly common, and many schools will likely begin using them for teaching students.

    a. Virtual reality headsets are important to the education of our students today, so they are becoming more common in schools.

    b. Students are finally learning how to use virtual reality headsets, so their costs are decreasing.

    c. Because virtual reality headsets are more affordable, students will see them more frequently in their classes.

3. Ending the era of silent movies, *The Jazz Singer* was the first "talkie" film in which actors spoke their lines rather than mouthing them.

Paraphrase: _____

_____

_____

4. According to Wikipedia, the sport of curling originated in the 16th century in Scotland with games first played in the winter on frozen ponds and lakes.

Paraphrase: _____

_____

_____

Fig 6.2 Reducing Waste: How You Can Help

AT A STORE	AT A RESTAURANT
Make careful decisions about what and how much you buy at the grocery store.	Reduce waste when eating in restaurants.
• Shop at stores that offer misshapen food at a discount.	• Skip the cafeteria tray. You will waste less if you carry your plates in your hands.
• Purchase prepared meals, which allow supermarkets to make use of imperfect produce.	• Take home leftovers.
• Buy frozen foods, which suffer fewer losses from farm to shelf.	• Share side dishes to keep portions under control.
• Shop often. Buy a few days' worth of produce at a time.	• Ask the waiter to hold extras such as bread and butter that you do not plan to eat.
• Buy fresh food at local farmers markets.	• Encourage restaurants and caterers to donate leftovers.

WRITING

ACTIVITY 17 | Follow the writing process to write a reaction essay

Step 1: Choose a prompt

Choose a prompt that you can react to. Your teacher may assign a prompt, you may think of one yourself, or you may choose one from the suggestions below.

- a video game you have played
- a concert or other live event you have attended
- a recent news story you have read
- a photograph
- Figure 6.2

1. What prompt did you choose? _____

2. How well do you know this prompt? What is your experience with it? Do you need to do more research on the prompt?

   _____

AT HOME	IN YOUR COMMUNITY
Small changes in the kitchen can reduce the amount of food your household throws out.	Businesses, schools, nonprofits, and governments can all find ways to dump less food.

AT HOME

Small changes in the kitchen can reduce the amount of food your household throws out.

- Use apps for food-expiration reminders.
- Switch to smaller dishes to control portions.
- Eat leftovers on a regular night each week.
- Give uneaten food a second chance. Freeze or can extras. Blend bruised fruit into smoothies.
- Try not to waste water-intensive foods like meat.

IN YOUR COMMUNITY

Businesses, schools, nonprofits, and governments can all find ways to dump less food.

- Ask your school to teach cooking, canning, and storage basics.
- Ask your local government for a curbside food-scrap collection service.
- Share extra produce from your home garden with your community.

Step 2: Brainstorm

Use the space below or a separate piece of paper to brainstorm your reactions to the prompt.

As you expected:

1. _____

2. _____

3. _____

Surprises:

1. _____

2. _____

3. _____

Step 3: Outline

On a separate piece of paper, write an outline to help you create a more detailed plan for your essay. Use your ideas from Step 2. Then exchange your outline with a partner. Use the Peer Editing Form 1 for Outlines in the *Writer's Handbook* to help you comment on your partner's work. Use your partner's feedback to revise your outline.

Step 4: Write the first draft

Use your outline and the feedback received to write the first draft of your reaction essay.

Step 5: Get feedback from a peer

Exchange your first draft with a partner. Use Peer Editing Form 6 in the *Writer's Handbook* to help you comment on your partner's writing.

Step 6: Reread, rethink, rewrite

Use the feedback to identify where you could improve your essay. Then write as many drafts as necessary to produce a good essay. Remember to proofread your essay before you submit it to find any errors.

Step 7: Write the final draft

Additional Topics for Writing

Here are five more topics for writing a reaction essay. Your teacher may require you to consult one or more sources.

TOPIC 1: A building in your city

TOPIC 2: A famous painting or other piece of art

TOPIC 3: An online blog entry

TOPIC 4: A music video

TOPIC 5: The lyrics to a song

TEST PREP

Write an essay about the following topic. Spend about 40 minutes on this task.

Think about a website or app you have used for learning English. Write an essay in which you briefly explain the website or app and then give your reaction(s) to it.

For this assignment, remember to double-space your essay. Include a short introduction with a thesis statement, two to four body paragraphs, and a brief conclusion. Write at least 300 words.

TIP

Avoid using phrases such as "I think . . ." or "I believe . . ." Instead of writing a sentence like "I believe that cats are better pets than canaries," you can simply write, "Cats are better pets than canaries." It is understood that this is your opinion, so you do not need to use opinion phrases.

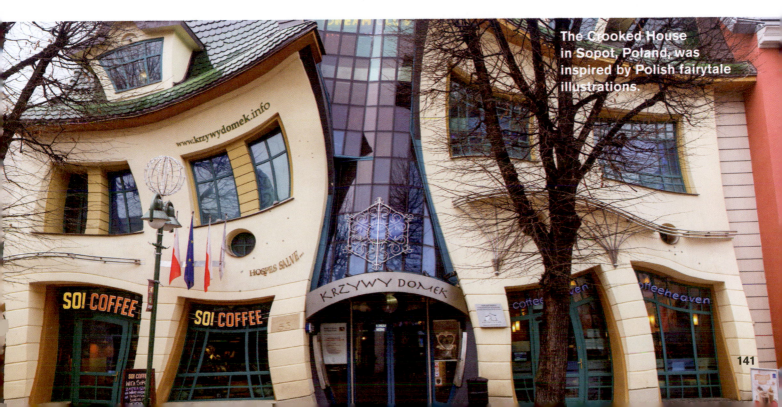

The Crooked House in Sopot, Poland, was inspired by Polish fairytale illustrations.

141

7 | Argument Essays

OBJECTIVES
- Review the structure of an argument essay
- Use transitions in argument writing
- Use modals in argument writing
- Use adverbs of degree
- Write an argument essay

A hissing cougar prowls the "Louisiana Swamp," at the Audubon Zoo in New Orleans, USA in a display designed for indigenous animals. The cat, a stand-in for a related subspecies that once roamed the Southeast, is now endangered and found only in Florida.

FREEWRITE | Look at the photo and read the caption. On a separate piece of paper, write your thoughts on whether animals should be kept in zoos.

ELEMENTS OF GREAT WRITING

What Is an Argument Essay?

We often try to persuade others to agree with our viewpoints, such as which movie to watch or where to go on vacation. In an **argument essay** (sometimes referred to as a persuasive essay), writers attempt to convince their readers to agree with them. By explaining their reasons for an opinion, they hope to convince others to share their point of view or to take a particular action.

One type of argument essay is a newspaper or magazine editorial, in which a writer chooses an issue and explains its relevance to readers to create a community of like-minded thinkers. For example, an editorial writer might endorse a particular candidate in an election, with the hope of persuading readers to vote for the candidate. Reading editorials in newspapers or online news sites can help you become familiar with the style and organization of good argument writing.

Another type of argumentation appears in online blogs. A blogger often explains his or her reasons for supporting or disagreeing with a certain issue. Of course, not all blog entries use persuasive writing, but some are good examples with well-supported opinions.

Well-written argument essays clearly and logically explain the writer's reasons for a particular viewpoint. However, writers should not exaggerate their claims. It is better to present the limitations of a viewpoint rather than overstate the case. If the writer's arguments seem exaggerated, readers will not accept the ideas. Good argument writing is not just personal opinions. Writers build more credible arguments when they cite respected sources to support their claims.

Organizing an Argument Essay

Your goal in an argument essay is to convince readers that your opinion about an issue is valid. To do this, you must state your opinion clearly in the **thesis statement**. However, the essay needs to be balanced to show that you understand the issue completely. One way to do this is to include an opposing viewpoint, or **counterargument**. Discussing only your opinion makes the essay sound biased, and readers may not be convinced of your viewpoint.

An argument essay has at least four paragraphs, but of course it could be longer. A typical five-paragraph argument essay has:

- an introductory paragraph that introduces the topic and thesis statement
- two body paragraphs that support the thesis statement
- a third body paragraph that includes a counterargument and a refutation
- a conclusion that summarizes the main points of the argument and restates the thesis

Here is an outline for a five-paragraph essay that argues that people should recycle daily.

INTRODUCTION	Paragraph 1	Hook Connecting information Thesis: Everyone should make recycling part of their daily life.
BODY	Paragraph 2	Support 1: Recycling saves energy. • Creating glass from recycled glass uses 50 percent less energy than making new glass. • Recycling one aluminum can saves enough energy to run a TV for three hours.
	Paragraph 3	Support 2: Recycling reduces air pollution. • Recycling prevents the emission of many greenhouse gases.
	Paragraph 4	Opposing viewpoint(s) • Counterargument: One person cannot make a difference. • Refutation: Each person produces 1,600 pounds of waste each year, but as much as 1,100 pounds of that total could be recycled.
CONCLUSION	Paragraph 5	Restated thesis Suggestion, opinion, or prediction

WRITER'S NOTE Using Persuasion

Many essay types—process, comparison, cause-effect, and reaction—can be seen as argument essays. For example, a process essay could attempt to persuade the reader that the process being described is the most appropriate way to achieve a desired result. A comparison essay might recommend one choice above another and use the comparison points as arguments. A cause-effect essay could argue that an event or course of action is harmful because of its effects. When you write in any rhetorical mode, persuasion can be one of your goals.

Bags of recyclables hang from a vendor's food cart in New York City.

Topics for Argument Essays

What is a suitable topic for an argument essay? Obviously, it should be an issue that you feel strongly about, know something about, and want to share your opinions on. When selecting a topic for this type of essay, consider relevant questions such as:

- How much do you know about this topic?
- Do you have an opinion on the topic? Why do you feel this way?
- Does the topic have two (or more) viewpoints? A topic without at least two viewpoints is not suitable.
- Can the topic generate more than just a personal opinion? For example, "chocolate is the best flavor" is not a good topic because it cannot be argued.

Read the list of general topics that lend themselves to an argument essay:

GENERAL TOPICS FOR ARGUMENT	
limiting oil exploration in environmentally sensitive areas	requiring future parents to take parenting classes
legalizing capital punishment	raising the driving age
mandating military service	using animals for medical research
requiring school uniforms	getting rid of zoos
banning cigarettes	restricting video games

ACTIVITY 1 | Identifying topics for argument essays

Check (✓) the four topics that are appropriate for an argument essay. Add two more topics for an argument essay.

_____ **1.** The first time someone flew in a plane

_____ **2.** The choice of a specific candidate to vote for in an election

_____ **3.** How and why birds migrate south for the winter

_____ **4.** Steps in negotiating an international contract

_____ **5.** The necessity of higher taxes on gasoline

_____ **6.** Why schools should offer after-school programs for at-risk students

_____ **7.** Reasons that you deserve a pay raise

_____ **8.** How to play chess well

9. _____

10. _____

Supporting Details

After selecting a topic, think about what you already know about the issue and what you need to find out. Asking yourself questions about both sides of an issue is a good way to generate ideas.

When brainstorming for an argument essay, a useful technique is to fill in a T-chart with the pro points in favor of and the con points against the topic. Here is an example of a pro-con T-chart.

Topic: Mandatory voting for all citizens over eighteen

PRO	CON
• In a democracy, everyone should participate. • Many people have died in wars so that we are able to vote. • If everyone votes, then the chosen candidate will represent the whole country.	• In a democracy, people should have the right to vote as well as not to vote. • Some people do not know the candidates and cannot make an informed choice.

ACTIVITY 2 | Brainstorming supporting ideas

For each topic, write two more pro ideas and two more con ideas.

1. *Topic:* Requiring future parents to take parenting classes

PRO	CON
• Parents will learn what babies need. • _____ _____ • _____ _____	• If a couple has not taken a class, you cannot stop them from having a baby. • _____ _____ • _____ _____

2. *Topic:* Allowing the death penalty

PRO	CON
• Criminals will not hurt innocent people again. • _____ _____ • _____ _____	• Countries that have the death penalty are not free of crime. • _____ _____ • _____ _____

A girl takes her cat for a walk.

3. *Topic:* Getting a pet for a child

PRO	CON
• Having a pet teaches a child responsibility.	• A child may mistreat a pet.
• _____	• _____
_____	_____
• _____	• _____
_____	_____

ACTIVITY 3 | Studying an example argument essay

Discuss the questions below with a partner. Then read Essay 7.1 and answer the questions that follow.

1. If you were going to complete a semester abroad, where would you want to go? Why?

2. What are reasons a student should study abroad? What are reasons that a student should not study abroad? Complete the T-chart with two to three points for and against.

Topic: Studying abroad for one semester

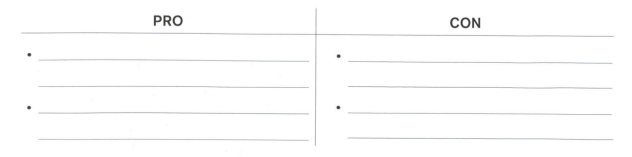

PRO	CON
• _____	• _____
_____	_____
• _____	• _____
_____	_____

ESSAY 7.1 **MLA**

Why Studying Abroad Is the Best Classroom

1   A British politician recently said, "In this age of growing interconnectedness, we understand that turning our backs on the world is simply not an option." Because of the rise of the Internet, the ease of global travel, and the increase in international trade, the world is more interconnected than ever before. In the past, people could enjoy a successful career without ever moving from their home region, but now many jobs involve global interactions. Given these new conditions, it is essential that college and university students experience new cultures as part of their education. Colleges and universities should require students to study abroad for at least one semester of their undergraduate education to prepare them for today's interconnected world.

2   One of the primary reasons that studying abroad contributes so effectively to students' education is that it requires them to live and learn in a culture that is different from their own. Correspondingly, in their analysis of the educational benefits of study-abroad programs, Brewer and Cunningham conclude that real learning is often **triggered** by a serious dilemma that causes the individuals involved to question **assumptions** they may have held for their entire lives (9). As Brewer and Cunningham demonstrate, students' daily assumptions are challenged by the experience of living abroad, from simple concerns, such as appropriate breakfast foods, to more complex matters, such as how societies should be organized and other cultural conventions. By experiencing a new culture firsthand, students will better appreciate the unique features of both their host and their home countries, as well as better understand the repercussions[1] of these cultural differences.

[1]repercussion: a negative result that was not expected

A Chinese college student participates in a study abroad experience at Yale University, Connecticut, USA.

3   Furthermore, studying abroad facilitates learning a new language. While studying the language before going abroad establishes a **framework** for future success, few experiences enhance language learning more than living in a country where it is used. As Kauffmann, Martin, and Weaver state, "Foreign settings offer many new resources for instruction, practice, and evaluation. Teaching methods that take advantage of the local environments can certainly be expected to improve on classroom methods" (36). For example, in a classroom, students might practice ordering food at a restaurant or asking directions to a museum; when studying abroad, however, they will have to use these skills in real-world situations.

4   Additionally, students benefit from studying their academic discipline from a new perspective. At first, this argument may appear illogical: Math is math, whether in Peru or Poland, and the fundamental principles of chemistry do not change from Ghana to Germany. Still, the ways in which disciplines are organized and taught may vary **considerably**, and students will see their discipline **in a new light** if it is taught in even a slightly different method. Learning to see the ways in which knowledge itself is organized can be one of the greatest benefits of studying abroad.

5   Though studying abroad offers many advantages, some may argue that a semester or year abroad is nothing but a vacation. While it is true that some students treat studying abroad as time off, the actions of a few students should not **invalidate** study abroad programs or cause colleges to abandon them. In fact, in a long-term study of 3,400 students, Dwyer and Peters found that a large number said studying abroad had an impact on their world view (96 percent), increased their self-confidence (96 percent), and gave them the skill set they needed for the career they chose (76 percent). Clearly, studying abroad is not just a party. Students' home institutions should offer preparatory workshops and orientation seminars so that students are ready for the requirements of the program and will better understand how it connects with their current academic work. Studying abroad unites academic demands with the thrill of discovering a new culture, and students will gain much more from the experience if they are prepared.

6   Given the numerous benefits of studying abroad, colleges and universities should require that their students take advantage of this opportunity, while also doing everything possible to keep these experiences affordable through reduced tuition and **subsidized** fees. It is essential that students learn to negotiate our increasingly interconnected world by exploring new cultures as part of their education. In a world made smaller by technological advances, students who graduate with the experience of living in a foreign culture will also be better prepared to succeed in their careers.

Works Cited

Brewer, Elizabeth, and Kiran Cunningham. "Capturing Study Abroad's Transformative Potential." *Integrating Study Abroad into the Curriculum: Theory and Practice across the Disciplines*, edited by Elizabeth Brewer and Kiran Cunningham, Stylus, 2009, pp. 1–29.

Dwyer, Mary, and C. Peters. "The Benefits of Study Abroad." *Transitions Abroad*, vol. 27, no. 5, 2004, pp. 56–57.

Kauffmann, Norman, Judith Martin, and Henry Weaver, with Judy Weaver. *Students Abroad, Strangers at Home: Education for a Global Society*. Intercultural Press, 1992.

1. What is the purpose of the essay? Begin your answer with *The purpose of* …

    _____

    _____

2. Underline the writer's thesis statement.

3. What arguments does the writer give to support his or her viewpoint?

    _____

    _____

4. Which paragraph gives an opposing idea? _____

    What is the opposing idea? _____

5. Do you agree with the thesis? If you disagree, what could the writer have done to make the point more convincing? If you agree, what are some ways in which the writer could have been even more convincing?

    _____

    _____

6. Does the last sentence in the conclusion offer a suggestion, an opinion, or a prediction?

    _____

ACTIVITY 4 | Analyzing the organization

Complete the outline using information from Essay 7.1.

Title: Why Studying Abroad Is the Best Classroom

I. Introduction

   A. Hook:

   B. People's jobs now depend on international connections.

   C. Thesis statement: Colleges and universities should require students to study abroad.

II. Body Paragraph 1

   A. Show how studying abroad lets students experience a foreign culture.

   B. Brewer and Cunningham (2009): _____

     _____

III. Body Paragraph 2

    A. Discuss how studying abroad contributes to learning a foreign language.

    B. Kauffmann, Martin, and Weaver (1992): _____

_____

IV. Body Paragraph 3

    A. Explain how studying abroad allows students to see their academic discipline from a new perspective.

    B. Provide a counterargument: _____

_____

V. Body Paragraph 4

    A. Address a common opposing idea that studying abroad is just a vacation.

    B. Show that A is not accurate. Study by: _____

    C. Argue that schools need to prepare their students for study abroad so they know the requirements and goals.

VI. Conclusion

    A. Suggest that studying abroad should be required.

    B. Opinion: _____

_____

Thesis Statements for Argument Essays

A thesis statement for an argument essay must clearly state the writer's position on a real issue. It should not be a personal opinion that cannot be proven, like "Popcorn is more delicious than peanuts." It often includes a word or phrase that signals an opinion _(should, ought to, need to, have an obligation to, must)_. In addition, it may include phrases such as, "for a number of reasons" and "because of several factors," that preview the reasons to be discussed. The most explicit thesis statement states the reasons the writer will use to support her argument. Study these examples:

Poor: Cigarette smoking in public places is not a very good idea.
          (Does not clearly state what the writer's position actually is.)

Good: Cigarette smoking in public places **should be banned**.
          (States clearly what the writer's position actually is.)

Better: Cigarette smoking in public places **should be banned because of several important reasons**.
          (Mentions that there are reasons to support the writer's position.)

Best: Cigarette smoking in public places **should be banned because of the health dangers it presents to not only smokers but also to people around them.**
          (Includes the writer's reasons.)

ACTIVITY 5 | Writing thesis statements for argument essays

Write a pro thesis statement and a con thesis statement for each topic from Activity 2.
When you finish, compare your answers with a partner's.

1. *Topic:* Requiring future parents to take parenting classes

   Pro thesis statement: _____

   _____

   Con thesis statement: _____

   _____

2. *Topic:* Allowing the death penalty

   Pro thesis statement: _____

   _____

   Con thesis statement: _____

   _____

3. *Topic:* Getting a pet for a child

   Pro thesis statement: _____

   _____

   Con thesis statement: _____

   _____

A couple with their children, Venice, Italy

Adding Counterargument and Refutation Statements

To persuade the reader that a viewpoint is correct, the writer needs to include strong support. Another technique is to include a **counterargument**—an opposing viewpoint. The counterargument allows the writer to admit a potential flaw in her argument and then to address it. Introducing this counterargument adds credibility to an essay. It shows that the writer understands more than one point of view about the topic. After providing a counterargument, the writer must give a **refutation**—a response to the counterargument—that either disproves it or shows it to be less convincing than the thesis.

Imagine that you are having an argument with a friend who disagrees with your opinion. What do you think will be the strongest argument against your point of view? That is your counterargument. How will you respond to the counterargument? The answer is your refutation.

Look at the following example. The counterargument is in italics and the refutation is underlined.

Some might say that in a democracy people should have the right to vote as well as not to vote. <u>However, if few people vote, then the chosen candidate may not represent the whole electorate.</u>

As you can see, what begins as a counterargument ends up as another reason in support of the writer's opinion.

Transitions for Counterarguments and Refutations

Here are some common transitions for developing support in your argument and for addressing a counterargument.

TRANSITIONS		EXAMPLES
Adding Supporting Information		
additionally	moreover	**What is more**, visits to the vet are extremely expensive.
furthermore	similarly	
in a similar way	what is more	
likewise		
Adding a Counterargment		
although	though	**Some might say** owning a pet is too expensive.
even though	while (it is true that)	**Although** owning a pet is expensive, cost should not be the main consideration.
some might say/argue		
Adding a Refutation		
despite (this)	nevertheless	Some might say owning a pet is too expensive. **Nonetheless**, it is wrong to put a dollar value on the joy pets bring.
however	nonetheless	
in fact	on the other hand	Although owning a pet is expensive, cost should not be the main consideration. **In fact**, it is wrong to put a dollar value on the joy pets bring.
in spite of (this)	yet	

ACTIVITY 6 | Identifying transitions

Reread Essay 7.1. Highlight the transitions used to add information.

ACTIVITY 7 | Identifying counterargument and refutation

Reread Essay 7.1 and complete the tasks.

1. Write the counterargument(s) used by the writer. _____

_____

2. Paraphrase the refutation used by the writer. _____

_____

ACTIVITY 8 | Writing refutations for counterarguments

For each counterargument, write a one-sentence refutation. Include different transition words for each item.

1. *Topic:* Mandatory retirement for pilots
   Thesis statement: Pilots should be required to retire at age 60 to ensure the safety of passengers.
   Counterargument: Some people may believe that older pilots' experience can contribute to flight safety.

   Refutation: _____

   _____

2. *Topic:* Food waste
   Thesis statement: As much as possible, people should not waste food.
   Counterargument: Food is inevitably lost during the harvesting and production process, and it is unrealistic to think that no food will be wasted.

   Refutation: _____

   _____

3. *Topic:* Teachers' salaries
   Thesis statement: Teachers' salaries should be tied to their students' test scores.
   Counterargument: Some people may believe that a teacher's role in a student's test score is not that important.

   Refutation: _____

   _____

ACTIVITY 9 | Choosing transitions

Discuss the questions below with a partner. Then read Essay 7.2, underline the appropriate transition, and answer the questions that follow.

1. What do you think *overfishing* means? Do a quick Internet search for the term *overfishing*. Write three facts that you learn.

2. What are some possible solutions to the problem of overfishing?

WORDS TO KNOW Essay 7.2

collapse: (n) destruction, breakdown
compensate for: (v phr) to make up for
compound: (v) to make something worse
deplete: (v) to decrease
downplay: (v) to minimize the importance of something
enclosed: (adj) surrounded

gravity: (n) seriousness
incentive: (n) a reason or motivation to do something
revolutionize: (v) to change in a significant way
suspend: (v) to stop something, usually for a short time
sustainable: (adj) able to continue to use longer

ESSAY 7.2   MLA

Empty Oceans

1 Imagine going to a sushi restaurant that could no longer serve fish. Such a scenario may seem unrealistic, but the fish populations of the earth's oceans face severe threats. Like land animals that have been hunted to near extinction, such as buffalo, elephants, and tigers, marine animals also need to be protected if they are to survive into future generations. Governments must encourage **sustainable** fishing practices and other regulatory guidelines to ensure that the oceans preserve their variety of animal and plant life as well as sufficient fish populations.

A scuba diver swimming past wall of jacks, Cocos Island, Costa Rica

2   The oceans are being **depleted** primarily due to consumer demand for seafood, which creates a financial **incentive** for marine businesses to overfish. As National Geographic documents, "Demand for seafood and advances in technology have led to fishing practices that are depleting fish and shellfish populations around the world. Fishers remove more than 77 billion kilograms of wildlife from the sea each year" ("Sustainable Fishing," n.d.). Similarly, in their research, Pichegru and colleagues concluded that "the development of industrial fishing in the twentieth century has reduced the total number of predatory fish globally to less than ten-percent of pre-industrial levels . . . and profoundly altered marine environments" (117). Because of this reduction, many species cannot reproduce quickly enough to **compensate for** the numbers that have been removed, which further **compounds** the problem.

3   [1] (Despite / What is more,) shifting ocean environments have made it difficult for many fish to find enough prey to feed on, and without a sufficient food supply, their population growth can be severely limited. Overfishing causes many other problems in the oceans. Changing the oceanic environment drastically multiplies the challenges that sea creatures face, as evidenced by such factors as the **collapse** of coral reefs in oceans throughout the world.

4   [2] (As a result / While) some people may **downplay** the problem of overfishing of our oceans, the statistics confirm its **gravity**. Stronger government controls of the fishing industry would help limit overfishing. [3] (Additionally / On one hand), tax breaks could be given to companies that operate fish farms, which is perhaps one of the simplest solutions to this problem. Rather than taking fish and shellfish from the ocean, fish farmers build **enclosed** facilities, such as tanks and aquariums, to raise these animals. [4] (Before / While) fish farming may be unfamiliar to many people, the practice dates back to 2000 BCE in China, and training manuals include a 475 BCE essay on raising carp by Fan Lai (Shepherd and Bromage, 2). With modern advances in technology, fish farming promises to **revolutionize** how humans fish.

5   [5] (Because / Some might argue that) the oceans are so huge that there must be plenty of fish left. [6] (Because / Nevertheless,) the fish in our oceans are in real trouble. In 1992, the United Nations Conference on Environment and Development defined the goal of sustainable development as meeting the "needs of the present without limiting the ability of future generations to meet their own needs" (Caulfield, 167). Without practical responses to the issue of sustainable fishing, including the necessity of **suspending** certain fishing practices and monitoring the health of the oceans, the planet risks losing many species of marine wildlife. By limiting fishing in the oceans and developing commercial fish farms, we can succeed in both raising fish for human consumption and preserving fish for the future.

Works Cited

Caulfield, Richard. *Greenlanders, Whales, and Whaling: Sustainability and Self-Determination in the Arctic.* University Press of New England, 1997.

National Geographic Education. "Sustainable Fishing." http://education.nationalgeographic.com/education/ encyclopedia/sustainable-fishing/?ar_a=1. Accessed 4 Mar. 2019.

Pichegru, L., P. Ryan, R. van Eeden, T. Reid, D. Grémillet, and R. Wanless. "Industrial Fishing, No-Take Zones, and Endangered Penguins." *Biological Conservation* vol. 156, 2012, pp. 117-25.

Shepherd, Jonathan. and Niall. Bromage. *Intensive Fish Farming.* Blackwell Science, 1992.

1. What is the purpose of the essay? Begin your answer with *The purpose of* ...

_____

_____

2. Underline the writer's thesis statement.

3. What counterargument does the writer provide?

_____

_____

4. Do you agree with the thesis? If you disagree, what could the writer have done to make the point more convincing? If you agree, what are some ways in which the writer could have been even more convincing?

_____

_____

_____

Grammar: Modals

Modals are auxiliary verbs that perform various functions—such as expressing ability, possibility, or obligation. Modals are helpful in argument essays because they can show a clear opinion about the topic. For example, the modals *must* and *have to* strongly assert a point and tell readers that something has to happen. Although *should* is not as strong as *must* or *have to*, it gives a clear recommendation and is therefore often used in argument essays. In addition, writers may use modals such as *may* and *might* to weaken a counterargument.

MODAL	PURPOSE	EXAMPLES
ought to should	To say what is the correct course of action	The government **ought to** realize that their tax plan will be bad for the economy. The sale of cigarettes **should** be banned immediately.
should	To give advice or a suggestion	People **should** take a few minutes every day to relax.
could may might	To show possibility	Students' test scores **may** increase if they spend at least 30 minutes per day writing.
have to must	To express necessity	For these reasons, the minimum age to obtain a driver's license **must** be raised immediately.

ACTIVITY 10 | Working with modals

Circle the most appropriate modals to complete Paragraph 7.1. More than one answer may be possible.

PARAGRAPH 7.1

The Key-Word Method

Students [1] (must / should) remember a lot of new words to be successful language learners. One technique that students [2] (should / must) try is the "key-word method." In this technique, learners [3] (might / should) first select a word in their native language that looks or sounds like the target English word. Then they [4] (must / should) form a mental association or picture between the English word and the native-language word. For example, an English speaker learning the Malay word for door, *pintu*, [5] (should / could) associate this target word with the English words *pin* and *into*. The learner then visualizes someone putting a "pin into a door" to open it, which [6] (must / might) help the learner to remember *pintu* for door. While it [7] (should / might) prove a time-consuming strategy for some learners, research on second-language learning shows that this technique consistently results in a very high level of learning. The "key-word" method is particularly effective in vocabulary acquisition.

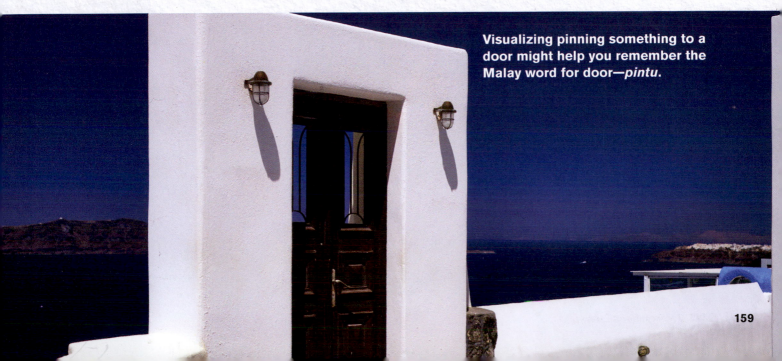

Visualizing pinning something to a door might help you remember the Malay word for door—*pintu*.

159

Grammar: Adverbs of Degree with Adjectives

One way to make your writing more precise is to use **adverbs of degree** to modify adjectives. Adverbs of degree give information about the extent of something. Many are used with particular adjectives. For example, you can say *incredibly excited* but not *completely excited*.

While *very* and *really* can be used with many adjectives, a common error is to overuse these adverbs in academic writing. It is important to use a variety of adverbs, not just these two.

Below are common academic adverbs of degree and the adjectives they often go with.

ADVERBS OF DEGREE		ADJECTIVES		EXAMPLES
exceptionally extremely fairly	immensely tremendously	angry difficult dull	exciting popular slow	The screenplay is **extremely** dull.
absolutely completely simply	totally utterly	amazing disgraceful disgusted disgusting	inaccurate unacceptable unpredictable	It is **absolutely** unacceptable for consumers to be treated this way.
deeply enormously	particularly profoundly thoroughly	concerning disappointed disappointing	disturbing upsetting	The latest jobs report is **deeply** disappointing.
highly		likely unlikely		It is **highly** likely that this great movie will win a lot of awards.
practically virtually		impossible		It is **practically** impossible to imagine a worse example of professional malpractice.

ACTIVITY 11 | Working with adverbs of degree

Unscramble the words and write each sentence correctly.

1. completely / the speaker's remarks / was / by / the audience / disgusted

_____

2. accurate / the medical tests / are / highly / used / heart disease / to diagnose

_____

3. is that it can be / about the weather / that we know / unpredictable / utterly / one thing

_____

4. is expensive / highly / to be / the drug / although / effective / it has proven

_____

5. to persuade / it can be / higher taxes / to vote for / difficult / citizens / extremely

_____

ACTIVITY 12 | Adding adverbs of degree

Complete each sentence with an appropriate adverb of degree. More than one answer is possible.

1. It is becoming _____ impossible to live without a cell phone these days.

2. Scientific breakthroughs into new cures for cancer are _____ slow in coming.

3. Investors will be _____ disappointed by the poor earnings report.

4. It is _____ believable how badly Puerto Rico was hit by Hurricane Maria in 2017.

5. The three new restaurants downtown feature an array of _____ amazing dishes.

6. It is _____ likely that many customer service jobs will disappear with the rise of artificial intelligence.

7. Unions representing pilots said that the pay cut proposed by the airline was _____ unacceptable.

A customer checks in at a "future hotel" by scanning his ID and face in Hangzhou, China. These hotels use AI to automate hotel services.

BUILDING BETTER VOCABULARY

ACTIVITY 13 | Word associations

Circle the word or phrase that is most closely related to the word or phrase on the left.

1.	collapse	destruction	slowly thinking
2.	compound	decrease	increase
3.	considerably	answer	greatly
4.	deplete	answer	finish
5.	downplay	less serious	more serious
6.	framework	plan	rehearsal
7.	gravity	amusement	seriousness
8.	in a new light	in a different way	in a different year
9.	suspend	stop for a time	wonder about
10.	trigger	use completely	cause to happen

ACTIVITY 14 | Collocations

Fill in the blank with the word that most naturally completes the phrase.

assumption	gravity	downplay	incentive	trigger

1. a(n) _____ to work hard

2. _____ the significance

3. make an incorrect _____

4. recognize the _____ of the situation

5. _____ an explosion

| collapse | considerably | invalidate | compensate | sustainable |

6. _____ for a weakness

7. a(n) _____ way of life

8. the _____ of the industry

9. _____ a contract

10. _____ more expensive

ACTIVITY 15 | Word forms

Complete each sentence with the correct word form. Use the correct form of the verbs.

NOUN	VERB	ADJECTIVE	ADVERB	SENTENCES
assumption	assume			**1.** Let's _____ that eating meat is detrimental to the planet. **2.** Residents thought the new budget included an increase for education, but this was an incorrect _____ .
consideration	consider	considerable considerate	considerably	**3.** A patient with this type of disease is usually in _____ pain. **4.** Vietnam produces _____ more coffee than Nicaragua or Honduras.
depletion	deplete	depleted		**5.** Fishermen know that the _____ of fish stock will adversely affect their businesses. **6.** The recent drought has left many reservoirs severely _____ of water.
revolution	revolutionize	revolutionary		**7.** We are seeing a _____ in the auto industry with the advent of self-driving cars. **8.** Scientists claim that the drug is _____ in its ability to combat cancer.
sustainability	sustain	sustainable sustained	sustainably	**9.** Economists are questioning the _____ of high growth rates in some parts of the world. **10.** Conservative investors put their money into companies whose growth is _____ over the long term.

Aquaculture—shown at a fish farm in Hawaii—is a sustainable form of fishing.

ACTIVITY 16 | Vocabulary in writing

Choose five words from Words to Know. Write a complete sentence with each word.

1. _____

2. _____

3. _____

4. _____

5. _____

BUILDING BETTER SENTENCES

ACTIVITY 17 | Editing

Each sentence has two errors. Find and correct them.

1. While most country around the world require a person to be at the least 18 years old to obtain a driver's license, in some parts of the United States and Canada, the minimum age is as young as 14.

2. One way to minimize the number of people they catch a cold each year is to encourage them to wash their hands frequent.

3. *Harry Potter and the Cursed Child*, the play that continues J. K. Rowling's famous fantasy series, begin 19 years after the events of last book in the series, *Harry Potter and the Deathly Hallows*.

4. Banjos and guitars are similar musical instrument, but banjos typically have four or five strings, whereas guitars typically they have six.

5. One of the earliest educational video game, *The Oregon Trail*, which first appeared in 1971, allows students learn about life as 19th-century American pioneers.

ACTIVITY 18 | Combining sentences

Combine the ideas into one sentence. You may change the word forms, but do not change or omit any ideas. There is more than one answer.

1. Flights are delayed.
   This happens often.
   These flights depart from San Francisco.
   These delays happen because of the fog.
   The fog is unpredictable.
   The fog blankets San Francisco.

   _____

   _____

2. Aretha Franklin was a singer.
   She was a songwriter.
   She played the piano.
   She was incredible.
   She died in 2018.

   _____

   _____

3. 51 million people live in the entire country of South Korea.
The majority of the population lives in the province surrounding Seoul.
Seoul is the capital of South Korea.

_____

_____

ACTIVITY 19 | Responding to teacher feedback

Read the teacher's comments on this first draft and rewrite the paragraph on a separate piece of paper.

PARAGRAPH 7.2 MLA

Spam

combine questions

How many emails do you receive every day that are unwanted offers? How many are

unwanted advertisements? Most of these emails are *spam*, commercial messages sent to a

word form

large number of recipient or posted in a large number of places. Spam, which Flynn and

Kahn define as "unsolicited email that is neither wanted nor needed" (179) by anyone, is

transition?

a huge problem today. Spam threatens the entire email system. Email is a vital method of

academic adverb

communication today, but the annoying mountain of spam threatens to destroy this really

fragment   *modal*

important tool. If email is to continue to be useful. Laws against spam may be strengthened

and enforced to avoid the exploitation of e-mail.

Street scene in South Korea

ACTIVITY 20 | Paraphrasing practice

For items 1 and 2, choose the best paraphrase of the sentence. For 3 and 4, write a paraphrase of the original sentence.

1. Astronomers argue whether Pluto, which was discovered in 1930 by Clyde Tombaugh, is really a planet or a dwarf planet.
   a. Astronomers argue about the value of Pluto.
   b. Clyde Tombaugh discovered Pluto in 1930, but astronomers disagree whether it is or is not a planet.
   c. Before 1930, Pluto was a dwarf planet, but with Clyde Tombaugh's help, it became a real planet in 1930.

2. The first gymnast to be awarded a perfect score of 10.0 at the Olympics, Romanian Nadia Comăneci won five gold medals during her famed career.
   a. Nadia Comăneci, a Romanian gymnast, was the first to earn a perfect score of 10.0 at the Olympics; she was awarded five gold medals during her gymnastics lifetime.
   b. Nadia Comăneci was a famous gymnast who won many gold medals.
   c. The Romanian gymnast Nadia Comăneci was the first to score a perfect 10.0 at the Olympics.

3. Cáo Xuĕqín, the Chinest poet, is the author of *Dream of the Red Chamber*, which is celebrated as one of the four great classical novels of Chinese literature.

   Paraphrase: _____

   _____

   _____

4. One of the most interesting sites in Abu Dhabi, Al Jahili Fort was built in 1891 to defend palm groves; local governors also resided there.

   Paraphrase: _____

   _____

   _____

WRITING

ACTIVITY 21 | Follow the steps to write an argument essay

Step 1: Choose a topic

Choose a topic that you can argue for or against. Your teacher may assign a topic, you may think of one yourself, or you may choose one from the suggestions below.

Humanities	Does every person have a moral responsibility to help the homeless?
Sciences	Is it right to use animals to test the safety of beauty and health products?
Business	Should the government increase the national minimum wage?
Sports	Are salaries of professional athletes too high?

1. What topic did you choose? _____

2. What is your experience with this topic? Do you need to do more research on the topic?

_____

Step 2: Brainstorm

Complete the T-chart with at least three pro ideas and three con ideas for your topic.

Topic: _____

PRO	CON

Step 3: Outline

On a separate piece of paper, write an outline to help you create a more detailed plan for your essay. Use your ideas from Step 2. Then exchange your outline with a partner. Use the Peer Editing Form 1 for Outlines in the *Writer's Handbook* to help you comment on your partner's work. Use your partner's feedback to revise your outline.

Step 4: Write the first draft

Use your outline and the feedback received to write the first draft of your argument essay.

Step 5: Get feedback from a peer

Exchange your first draft with a partner. Use Peer Editing Form 7 in the *Writer's Handbook* to help you to comment on your partner's writing.

Step 6: Reread, rethink, rewrite

Use the feedback to identify places where you could make revisions to improve your essay. Then write as many drafts as necessary to produce a good essay. Remember to proofread your essay before you submit it to find any errors.

Step 7: Write the final draft

Additional Topics for Writing

Here are five more ideas for topics for additional argument essay writing.

TOPIC 1: In many places, the minimum driving age is between 16 and 18, and drivers can keep their licenses as long as they are good drivers. Do you think there should be a maximum age after which a person can no longer keep a driver's license?

TOPIC 2: Should cities ban the use of plastic bags?

TOPIC 3: Should university-level education be free for students?

TOPIC 4: Is restricting gun ownership the best way to prevent violent crime?

TOPIC 5: Should junk food manufacturers be allowed to advertise their products to children?

TEST PREP

Write an argument essay about the following topic. You should spend about 40 minutes on this task.

Should people eat a vegetarian diet? Write an essay for or against vegetarianism.

For this assignment, remember to include a counterargument and refutation. Include a short introduction with a thesis statement, two to four body paragraphs, and a brief conclusion.

> **TIP**
>
> Researching topics helps you to compose more effective argument essays. Facts matter more than opinions in this type of essay, so the more evidence you use to support your viewpoint, the more convincing your claims will be.

A boy and his grandfather practice their driving skills.

8 | The Research Paper

OBJECTIVES
- Learn the steps in writing a research paper
- Practice the passive voice
- Write a research paper

A photo taken by astronaut Tim Peake on the International Space Station shows Viedma glacier in Patagonia, Argentina. Peake performed more than 30 scientific experiments during his six-month mission.

FREEWRITE | Look at the photo and read the caption. On a separate piece of paper, write about an area of research that you are interested in.

ELEMENTS OF GREAT WRITING

What Is a Research Paper?

A **research paper** is a long essay in which writers present their perspective on a topic using independent sources, including books, journal articles, and the Internet. In research papers, writers demonstrate their knowledge—and unique interpretation—of a topic.

Like essays, research papers usually begin with an introduction. This introduction typically consists of one paragraph but may have more than one, depending on the overall length of the paper. This introduction includes a thesis statement. Following the introduction are supporting paragraphs that develop and explore the thesis. Finally, the research paper finishes with a concluding section that summarizes the major points of the argument.

The key difference between an essay and a research paper is that a research paper includes information and data from other sources, whereas some essays do not. For research papers, writers must cite the work of various experts to support their interpretation of the topic.

Preparing to Write a Research Paper

Writing a research paper includes similar steps as writing an essay, but the most important step is researching the topic. You cannot write a research paper without conducting research.

The more information you gather about the topic before you start planning and writing, the better your paper will be, and the smoother the writing process will be. The steps of the writing process are outlined below, though they are not necessarily sequential.

Step 1: Understand the Assignment

Because teachers have different requirements for research papers, it is important to follow the assignment carefully. Consider these questions before starting an assignment:

1. Can you select your own topic? Or is there a specific topic? If so, are you allowed to modify the topic?

2. How long is the research paper expected to be? Sometimes the length is expressed in page length and other times in number of words.

3. How many outside sources are required? What types of sources are required? Is a specific number of any type of source required? For example, do you need at least one book and at least five journal articles? Are websites allowed as a source?

4. What type of citation is expected? APA? MLA? Chicago? Other?

5. What is the final due date for the completed paper? Are you expected to turn in parts of the paper on different dates? For example, some teachers require an outline by one date, a first draft by another, and a final draft by a later date.

6. What font and font size should be used? This is sometimes determined by the style your teacher wants (e.g., the recommended font for APA is 12-point Times New Roman).

7. Should the assignment be submitted in hardcopy, an electronic attachment, or both? If hardcopy, how many copies do you submit?

8. If there is a scoring rubric, read it carefully. The details in the rubric will indicate what the teacher expects so that you can achieve the best grade possible. If there is no rubric, ask your teacher how the paper will be graded.

Step 2: Choose a Topic

Often, teachers give specific topics to write about. For example, your teacher may limit the research paper to the topic of "The effects of high gasoline prices on the nation."

Alternatively, teachers may assign a general topic and allow students to determine the direction of the paper. For example, the teacher may assign the general topic of "Learning a foreign language," and you may choose the specific topic "Why English spelling is challenging for non-native speakers."

In some classes, teachers will describe the type of research paper and ask students to choose a suitable topic. For example, your teacher may give the assignment: "Select an historical event and compare the information in three different sources. Pay careful attention to the accuracy of the information and the objectivity of the author." In this case, you could address any historical event you think would be interesting to research and write about.

ACTIVITY 1 | Choosing research paper topics

Read each pair of topics and check (✓) which you think is the better choice for a research paper of 1,500 words with at least three cited sources. In some cases, neither example may be perfect. Discuss your answers with a partner.

1. _____ **a.** Astronomy

   _____ **b.** The naming of our planets

2. _____ **a.** How to achieve world peace

   _____ **b.** How Europe shaped the map of Africa

3. _____ **a.** The meaning of O. Henry's short story "The Gift of the Magi"

   _____ **b.** A comparison of works by O. Henry, William Shakespeare, and Stephen King

4. _____ **a.** A comparison of job opportunities for women in Europe in 1815, 1915, and 2015

   _____ **b.** The greatest achievements of Indian Prime Minister Indira Gandhi

5. _____ **a.** The salaries of current professional basketball players

   _____ **b.** The rules of basketball

Step 3: Brainstorm Questions about the Topic

As with essays, you should brainstorm ideas for a research paper. One way to brainstorm for a research paper is to come up with questions that the paper can answer for the reader. Look at the example below:

Research Topic	The effects of high gasoline prices on the nation
Possible Questions	What price is considered "high"? Why are gasoline prices high? What are the effects of high gasoline prices? Are these effects stronger or worse in certain areas of the nation? Which effect is the most serious? What can we do to reduce the price of gasoline? What can we do to reduce the effects of high gasoline prices?

ACTIVITY 2 | Brainstorming questions

For each topic, brainstorm ideas by writing three possible questions. Then discuss with a partner which topic you think would be the easiest to use for a research paper.

Research topic   The benefits of artificial intelligence

Possible questions   1. _____

2. _____

3. _____

Research topic   The connections between video games and teenage well-being

Possible questions   1. _____

2. _____

3. _____

Research topic   The causes of human migration

Possible questions   1. _____

2. _____

3. _____

The Rose Reading Room
at the New York Public Library,
New York City

Step 4: Evaluate Sources

Follow these steps when evaluating a source.

1. **Is the author a respected authority in the field?** Look for the author's university affiliation and professional associations. Many people on the Internet describe themselves as experts, but such claims must be verified.

2. **Is the publisher reputable?** University and academic presses publish high-quality material that has been peer-reviewed. For a source to be peer-reviewed, experts assess the merits of the paper before it is published, which ensures its quality. For this reason, a peer-reviewed publication is always preferred as a source. If you are using a website, make sure it is reputable. Government or educational sites—ones that have URLs sending in *.gov* or *.edu*— are usually reputable.

3. **Does the source contain any bias?** Bias is not necessarily disqualifying, but you need to determine whether the source favors a certain side of an issue. For example, if an article says that petroleum companies do not represent a danger to the environment, check what other sources are cited. If most of the sources are from oil companies, there is probably bias.

4. **Does the paper include citations?** Multiple citations indicate that the author's ideas are based on other people's ideas, too. Very few citations indicate that the source may represent the ideas of the author without giving proper consideration to other experts.

5. **How current is the information?** In general, sources should be within the past 10 years for subjects in which information changes quickly (science, technology, medicine). Sources may be older in fields such as the humanities. Consider whether the age of a source adversely affects its usefulness to your research. No matter what the date of publication is, it is your responsibility to be sure that all of your sources contain information that is relevant and accurate.

While a quick search on Wikipedia can provide some general background information, you will probably have to use more scholarly sources for your research paper.

One source that specializes in academic articles is Google Scholar (scholar.google.com). If you can identify one or two good scholarly articles, you can examine the bibliographies of those articles for other potential articles.

Another good source of scholarly work is your school's library website. This website will typically include specific databases that will allow you to focus exclusively on your topic.

Once you have found a credible source, use a chart to carefully note the information about that source so that you can find it again later. See the example below:

Topic: The War of 1812

TITLE	SOURCE	AUTHOR	YEAR	PAGE REFERENCE
"American Trade Restrictions during the War of 1812"	*The Journal of American History* (Volume 68, Number 3)	Donald Hickey	1981	517–38

ACTIVITY 3 | Finding sources for a research paper

For one of the topics in Activity 2, use Google Scholar to find three possible articles for a research paper. On a separate piece of paper, create a chart like the one above and complete it with information about your sources.

ACTIVITY 4 | Evaluating sources for a research paper

Look at your answers to Activity 3. Then answer the questions below.

1. Which is the best source? _____

   Why? _____

   _____

2. Which is the weakest source? _____

   Why? _____

   _____

ACTIVITY 5 | Understanding a reference list

Answer the questions about the reference list for a research paper in APA style.

References

Carrell, R. (1991). Second language reading: Reading ability or language proficiency. *Applied Linguistics, 12* (2), 159–179.

Chun, D., & Plass, J. (1996). Effects of multimedia annotations on vocabulary acquisition. *The Modern Language Journal, 80* (2), 183–199.

Clipperton, R. (1994). Explicit vocabulary instruction in French immersion. *The Canadian Modern Language Review/La Revue Canadienne des Langues Vivantes, 50,* 736–749.

Folse, K. (2004). *Vocabulary myths: Applying second language research to the classroom.* Ann Arbor: University of Michigan Press.

Huckin, T., & Coady, J. (1999). Incidental vocabulary acquisition in a second language. *Studies in Second Language Acquisition, 21,* 181–193.

Hulstijn, J. (1993). When do foreign-language readers look up the meaning of unfamiliar words? The influence of task and learner variables. *The Modern Language Journal, 77* (2), 139–147.

Jenkins, J., Matlock, B., & Slocum, T. (1989). Two approaches to vocabulary instruction: The teaching of individual word meanings and practice in deriving word meaning from context. *Reading Research Quarterly, 24* (2), 215–235.

Koda, K. (1996). L2 word recognition research: A critical review. *The Modern Language Journal, 80* (4), 450–460.

Laufer, B. (1990). Why are some words more difficult than others? *International Review of Applied Linguistics in Language Teaching, 28* (4), 293–307.

Laufer, B. (1998). The development of passive and active vocabulary in a second language: Same or different? *Applied Linguistics, 19* (2), 255–271.

Ott, C., Butler, D., Blake, R., & Ball, J. (1973). The effect of interactive-image elaboration on the acquisition of foreign language vocabulary. *Language Learning, 23* (2), 197–206.

1. How are the 11 sources arranged? _____

_____

2. Look at the first entry only. What is capitalized? _____

_____

3. Of these 11 sources, 10 are academic journals and 1 is a book. Which entry do you think is the book, and why? Hint: There are at least two differences in how a book and a journal article are listed. _____

_____

4. Which journals have more than one listing? _____

_____

5. Put a check mark (✔) next to the oldest and most recent articles.

6. How are multiple sources with the same author sequenced? _____

Step 5: Read and Take Notes

At this point, you need to read extensively. Be sure that you are reading a variety of sources by a variety of authors. You should also take notes. Some people underline, while others copy phrases or sentences in a notebook or online record holder. Some students prefer to highlight with different-colored markers, with each color connecting related topics and ideas. Use whatever note-taking techniques work best for you.

Step 6: Write a Thesis Statement

In the brainstorming step, you wrote questions that your paper might answer. Now you should develop a thesis statement that tells readers what your paper will teach them. A good thesis statement does not just present a fact. Instead, it must present a position.

Imagine a student in a literature course needs to write a research paper explaining a novel's message or value to society. The student chooses the classic children's story *Charlotte's Web* (E. B. White, 1952). Look at three possible thesis statements:

A sketch of the barn swing in E. B. White's *Charlotte's Web*

1. *Charlotte's Web* is an excellent children's book.

2. In *Charlotte's Web*, the author E. B. White depicts the meaning of friendship.

3. In *Charlotte's Web*, the author E. B. White suggests that true friendship includes sacrifice.

The first sentence gives an opinion, and a research paper should present ideas supported by facts, not opinions. Sentence 2 is a fact. It does not present a position, so it would not make a good thesis. Sentence 3 is the best thesis statement because it takes a position and is likely to make readers question the kind of sacrifice that friendship involves.

ACTIVITY 6 | Practicing writing thesis statements

Choose three topics from Activity 1. Write a thesis statement for each topic.

1. Topic: _____

   Thesis statement: _____

   _____

2. Topic: _____

Thesis statement: _____

_____

3. Topic: _____

Thesis statement: _____

_____

Step 7: Make an Outline

Follow the same steps for outlining as in the previous units of this book. Remember that the research paper includes an introductory paragraph (with a hook, connecting information, and thesis statement), body paragraphs that support and explain the thesis, and a conclusion that summarizes the argument in its entirety.

Step 8: Locate Specific Information for the Outline

Even though you have probably found some sources for parts of your outline, you should also identify parts of the argument that need more support. This is a good time to search for information to strengthen the weaker parts of your outline. This could involve reading sources you previously found again or seeking new sources.

Step 9: Organize Your Notes

Often researchers can feel overwhelmed by their notes, so it is a good idea to organize them as clearly as possible. Look for points of connection between your notes and your outline. Some people use different-colored highlighters to coordinate information.

For example, in the outline below, the main idea of the body paragraph and supporting ideas are highlighted in blue. The writer could also use yellow to highlight the quotations and information in his or her notes from Step 5.

II. Topic: Biographical details concerning Lafitte's early life are difficult to learn.

    A. Hart and Penman (2012) call him a "man of legend more than fact" (p. 199)

    B. His name invites debate—different spellings

    C. Most historians agree that Lafitte was born around 1780

    D. Historians disagree on his birthplace: Davis (2005)–Pauillac, France (p. 2); Ramsay (1996)–Saint-Domingue

Step 10: Write a First Draft with Cited Sources

Now that you have your outline and notes from your sources, it is time to write your first draft. This step is very similar to writing an essay, but now you must include specific information from your sources to support your ideas.

When you give information that is not your original work, you must cite it in the body of your paper. This means that you identify the original source that contained the information.

Before you start writing, check to see how many citations and which types of sources the assignment requires. Also check which style is required (APA, MLA, Chicago, etc.).

In APA style, there are three primary ways to include the author's name that you are citing:

1. Use the author's name and a reporting verb such as *says*, *explains*, or *reports*. (See Unit 3 for more information on reporting verbs.)

   Johnson (2011) explains that the war began because one country needed money.

2. Use the preposition *according to* plus the author's name or name of the source.

   According to Johnson (2011), the war began because one country needed money.

3. Cite the author's name in parentheses after the information.

   The war began because one country needed money **(Johnson, 2011).**

For more information on citing, see Unit 3 and Citing Sources in the *Writer's Handbook*.

In addition to providing in-text citations, you should also list all the works, or sources, in the References (APA) or Works Cited list (MLA) at the end of your paper.

Step 11: Get Feedback

All writers benefit from independent feedback. You can ask another student to read your paper. In some cases, your teacher will read your first draft and offer feedback.

Step 12: Revise the Outline and Write the Final Draft

If you receive feedback that suggests parts of your first draft are unclear, you may need to revise your outline. You may want to get more feedback from a second reviewer before you finalize your outline. Once you are satisfied that you have responded to reviewers' comments and that your outline is complete, you are ready to write the final draft.

WRITER'S NOTE Adding Headers

Because research papers are longer than essays, writers often use headers within the paper to help the reader better follow the information. Headers are like subtitles; they help to break the content into sections. Headers also help the writer make sure that all the information in a section relates to that specific topic.

ACTIVITY 7 | Analyzing an example research paper

Read the excerpt below from the beginning of Research Paper 8.1 and discuss the questions with a partner. Then read Research Paper 8.1 and answer the questions that follow.

> "Most battles are fought to win wars, and most wars are fought between armies, but the role of the pirate Jean Lafitte in the War of 1812 is an exception. The War of 1812 was between the United States of America and Great Britain, and it took place only a few decades after the United States declared its independence in 1776."

1. Do you think the War of 1812 was mostly fought on land or at sea? How do you know?

2. How do you think a pirate became involved in the War of 1812?

WORDS TO KNOW Research Paper 8.1

alliance: (n) a group of countries (political parties, people, etc.) joined for a purpose
ally: (n) a person, group, or country associated with another for a common purpose
commence: (v) to begin
diplomatic: (adj) related to the skill of managing international relations
flourish: (v) to succeed
fragile: (adj) weak, delicate
hostile: (adj) unfriendly, aggressive

inclination: (n) a tendency
join forces: (v phr) to team up, unite
legend: (n) a well-known story that cannot be verified
legitimate: (adj) legal, lawful; valid
margin: (n) an edge or outside limit
notorious: (adj) well-known due to bad deeds
spy: (n) a person who attempts to secretly discover information
ultimatum: (n) a final demand

A 19th century painting depicts the sinking of the *HMS Guerriere* by the *USS Constitution* during the War of 1812.

The Pirate's Unnecessary Battle: Jean Lafitte and the War of 1812

Jean Lafitte (1780–1826)

1   Most battles are fought to win wars, and most wars are fought between armies, but the role of the pirate Jean Lafitte in the War of 1812 is an exception. The War of 1812 was between the United States of America and Great Britain, and it took place only a few decades after the United States declared its independence in 1776. Lafitte was a **notorious** pirate and smuggler in the Gulf of Mexico, a man on the **margins** of society who played a critical role in the Battle of New Orleans. Oddly enough, that battle began after the United States and Great Britain had signed a treaty to end the war. Lafitte's efforts in the War of 1812 certainly helped to establish the United States as a world power, but history should neither overlook his criminality nor minimize his accomplishments.

Jean Lafitte: Life of a Pirate

2   Basic biographical details concerning Lafitte's early life are difficult to learn. Indeed, Hart and Penman (2012) call him a "man of **legend** more than fact" (p. 199) because, although numerous stories tell about his career as a pirate and a soldier, most of these accounts cannot be clearly documented. Even his name invites debate, with most sources using the English spelling (Lafitte) rather than the French spelling (Laffite). Most historians agree that Lafitte was born around 1780, but historians disagree on his birthplace. For example, Davis (2005) suggests that Lafitte's birthplace was Pauillac, France (p. 2), while Ramsay (1996) proposes he was likely born in the French colony of Saint-Domingue, which today comprises parts of the Dominican Republic and Haiti.

3   It is clear that Lafitte and his brother Pierre were engaged in piracy and smuggling in the late 1700s and early 1800s. Their father worked as a merchant, so it is likely that they spent their adolescent years near the sea and learned much about trade routes, international ports, and the economic potential of criminal activity. They arrived in New Orleans in the early 1800s and began trading with local merchants. A few years later, as tensions with Great Britain rose, the United States passed a law that prohibited American merchants from trading with unfriendly European nations. This law caused financial hardship for numerous businesses, both **legitimate** and criminal, and so the Lafitte brothers turned other people's difficulties into their economic gain.

4   After establishing their base on Barataria, a small island located south of New Orleans in Barataria Bay, the Lafitte brothers positioned themselves as the dominant pirates and smugglers of the region, including the profitable trade in New Orleans, which had long been one of the United States' busiest ports. With Pierre running their enterprise in New Orleans and Jean taking care of the daily operations in Barataria, the Lafitte brothers quickly became very rich and powerful while living under the shadow of the law and pursuing their criminal activities. The brothers controlled several ships and crews, which robbed other vessels, and they traded the stolen goods in New Orleans. Governors of Louisiana occasionally attempted to shut down the Lafittes' criminal operations, but without success, and many of the people of New Orleans supported the brothers' activities because they brought goods into the city that were forbidden by law. Given Jean Lafitte's illegal actions, it is rather surprising that he became a leading figure in the Battle of New Orleans and, for some, an American hero.

Lafitte's Role in the War of 1812

5   The War of 1812 began on June 18, 1812, after U.S. President James Madison and Congress declared war on Great Britain to protest a series of **hostile** actions, including harassment of American ships on the seas and minor battles fought over the Canadian border. Great Britain's navy was the strongest military force in the world at the time, so many people assumed that the American forces would be quickly crushed. Much of the War of 1812 was fought in the Atlantic Ocean and on the Canadian border in the Great Lakes region, but command of the Mississippi River was seen as critical for the United States to maintain its territories. In addition, whichever side controlled the Mississippi River and its numerous channels would also control its largest port, New Orleans, which was of incredible importance for sending supplies to troops. Given these strategic conditions, both American and British forces turned their attention to the Gulf of Mexico toward the end of the conflict. Both sides in the conflict also realized that if they desired to capture New Orleans, the pirate Jean Lafitte would be a valuable **ally**, and they sought to ensure that he would not remain neutral in the conflict.

6   The British attempted to gain the cooperation of Lafitte first by offering him assurances of their goodwill. According to Owsley (1981), "The first suggestion by the British that the Baratarians might **join forces** with them and allow use of the base at Barataria as a point of attack against New Orleans is found in Pigot's report to Admiral Cochrane dated June 8, 1814" (p. 108). Surely this offer must have been very tempting to Lafitte, for in the early 1800s the United Kingdom was by far the more powerful nation. Of French background by birth, Lafitte likely would not have felt much loyalty to the United States, and it is important to remember that Louisiana did not join the union until April 30, 1812, only a few months before the war began. Many historians debate Lafitte's reasons for not siding with the more powerful force of the war, and Latimer (2007) proposes: "The gang threw in their lot with the Americans only because they realized that the offer the British were making was, in fact, an **ultimatum**: The British were finally enforcing Spanish authority in the area on behalf of their ally" (p. 371). Also, while Louisiana had only recently joined the United States of America, this state had a rich French legacy, which might have influenced Lafitte's loyalties. Regardless of his reasons, Lafitte's decision to assist the United States played a crucial role in the Battle of New Orleans. The British would have likely won the battle with his assistance because the city would have been isolated from the interior (de Grummond, 1968). Given his knowledge of sea routes and Louisiana's marshy waterways, Lafitte would have been an invaluable ally for the British regime, and if New Orleans fell to the British, the war would likely have lasted much longer.

7   Nonetheless, the fact that Lafitte refused to cooperate with the British forces did not mean that he would join with the United States, or that the United States would desire to work with a pirate. Stagg (2012) describes how Andrew Jackson, who led the U.S. forces in the campaign, hesitated to enter into an **alliance** with Lafitte because doing so "went against his personal **inclinations**" (p. 152). Upon arriving in New Orleans, however, Jackson realized that the city lacked sufficient defenses to protect itself against a British invasion, and so drastic measures needed to be taken. To this end, Jackson realized that Lafitte's experience with ships, his knowledge of the region's geography, and the many men under his command would be great advantages for the United States in the coming battle. Lafitte negotiated with Jackson for the pardon of his men following the battle, and this **fragile** alliance between the U.S. military and a group of pirates began. The British fleet reached the Mississippi River on December 23, 1814, and hostilities began soon after.

8   With Lafitte's assistance and technical advice, particularly concerning the placement of American defenses, the United States had a decisive victory over the British—with the British reporting over 2,000 dead, whereas the Americans lost less than 100. However, it turned out that the Battle of New Orleans need not have been fought, and many soldiers lost their lives without reason. The Treaty of Ghent, which ended the war, was signed on December 24, 1814, with the Battle of New Orleans occurring on January 8, 1815. If communication had traveled more quickly in the early 1800s, the Battle of New Orleans would never have **commenced**, and thus Lafitte would not hold his place in American history. Moreover, neither the United States nor Great Britain gained any lasting advances through the war: "In strict military and **diplomatic** terms, the War of 1812 accomplished almost nothing. All that the United States had managed was to convince the British to return all territorial boundaries and diplomatic disputes to their prewar status" (Eustace, 2012, p. xi).

9   After his participation in the War of 1812, Lafitte again devoted his ambitions to piracy and, once again living in the criminal underworld, soon faded from public view. Wall (1997) documents that "federal officials forced Lafitte to move from Barataria Bay" and that he then "established a new headquarters on Galveston Island and continued his illegal slave business" (p. 97). Lafitte sided with Spain in the Mexican War of Independence. He recruited his brother Pierre, and together they acted as **spies** from their base in Galveston. However, in the following decades, governmental authorities largely freed the Gulf of Mexico from piracy, and Jean and Pierre Lafitte found themselves in an environment no longer friendly to their criminality: "The world they had known and in which they could hope to **flourish** had left them behind, and the new world of the Gulf simply had no room for their kind" (Davis, 2005, p. 467). Some historians think Lafitte changed his name and began a new life freed from his past, while others think he died in a battle at sea, possibly at the hands of his men who revolted against him.

Conclusion

10   So much remains unknown about Jean Lafitte's life, yet it is clear that he played a critical role in this unnecessary battle. He remains a man of legend, such as the longstanding belief, which lacks any evidence, that he rescued the exiled French emperor Napoleon Bonaparte and brought him safely to freedom in Louisiana. Indeed, he is a particularly celebrated figure in Louisiana, with the Jean Lafitte National Historical Park and Preserve named in his honor. Without strong support in history, however, the stories about such men as Lafitte are appealing but make it hard to distinguish fact from fiction. Considered a hero for his contributions to an unnecessary war, one cannot deny that Lafitte was also a criminal throughout much of his life.

References

Davis, W. (2005). *The pirates Laffite: The treacherous world of the corsairs of the Gulf.* Orlando, FL: Harcourt.

De Grummond, J. (1968). *The Baratarians and the Battle of New Orleans.* Baton Rouge, LA: Louisiana State University Press.

Eustace, N. (2012). *1812: War and the passions of patriotism.* Philadelphia, PA: University of Pennsylvania Press.

Hart, S., & Penman, R. (2012). *1812: A nation emerges.* Washington, DC: Smithsonian Institution.

Latimer, J. (2007). *1812: War with America.* Cambridge, MA: Belknap.

Owsley, F., Jr. (1981). *Struggle for the Gulf borderlands: The Creek War and the Battle of New Orleans, 1812-1815.* Gainesville: University of Florida Press.

Ramsey, J. (1996). *Jean Laffite: Prince of pirates.* Austin: Eakin.

Stagg, J. C. A. (2012). *The War of 1812: Conflict for a continent.* Cambridge: Cambridge University Press.

Wall, B., Ed. (1997). *Louisiana: A history* (3rd ed.). Wheeling, IL: Harlan Davidson.

1. What is the purpose of this research paper? Begin your answer with *The purpose of …*

_____

2. Underline the thesis statement.

3. Which paragraph gives background information? _____

4. How many headers are there? _____

5. How many different sources are used? _____

How many direct quotations are there? _____

Grammar: Passive Voice

We use the passive voice if we do not know who performed a particular action, or if the person performing the action is less important than the action itself. That is to say, when using the passive voice, the focus is on the action or the end result of the action, not the actor. The object of the verb in the active voice moves to the subject position in the passive voice.

object

Active: People **write** <u>Arabic</u> from left to right.

subject

Passive: <u>Arabic</u> **is written** from left to right.

object

Active: Government officials **have spent** <u>most of the money</u> on key resources.

subject

Passive: <u>Most of the money</u> **has been spent** on key resources.

In the passive voice examples on the previous page, it is not important who writes Arabic or who has spent the money. Instead, the passive voice focuses on the Arabic language and the money.

A passive verb consists of two parts: the verb *be* and the past participle of the verb. There are three tenses commonly used in the passive voice in academic writing—the simple present, simple past, and present perfect. Modals are also used. Note that only transitive verbs (verbs that take objects) can be made passive.

Simple Present:	Arabic **is written** from left to right.
Simple Past:	The United Nations **was established** soon after Word War II.
Present Prefect:	Most of the money **has been spent** on key resources.
Modal:	Popcorn **can be cooked** in a microwave very quickly.

ACTIVITY 8 | Writing passive voice sentences

Rewrite each sentence using the passive voice.

1. You can make a very simple soup with chicken, onions, tomatoes, water, salt, and pepper.

   _____

2. At midnight last night, senators were still considering the bill.

   _____

3. Several key countries, including Vietnam and Brazil, grow high-quality coffee.

   _____

4. This factory produces thousands of auto parts every week.

   _____

5. With any type of lettuce and some fresh vegetables, anyone can make a healthy salad quite easily.

   _____

6. For the past two weeks, many customers in the Toronto area have experienced serious problems with cell phone service.

   _____

7. Local governments created more than a dozen new voting districts in Tennessee in the 1970s.

   _____

8. Driving from Miami to New York exhausts most travelers.

   _____

ACTIVITY 9 | Using correct verb forms

Complete the paragraph with the correct tense and form (active or passive) of the verb in parentheses. More than one answer may be possible.

Online Courses

As computers [1] _____ (become) increasingly important in education, many more online courses [2] _____ (offer) by colleges and universities. In this new type of education, some students never even [3] _____ (set) foot on campus to earn a degree. Online learning [4] _____ (cause) a revolution in education, but its benefits need [5] _____ (measure) against its liabilities when it [6] _____ (compare) to traditional face-to-face instruction. Students should not [7] _____ (assume) that either online or face-to-face classes are superior. Instead, students should [8] _____ (pay) attention to the information they [9] _____ (need) from a particular course and which type of learning [10] _____ (facilitate) their education the best.

Students taking a class outside, South Africa

BUILDING BETTER VOCABULARY

WORDS TO KNOW

alliance (n) **AW**	fragile (adj)	legitimate (adj) **AW**
ally (n)	hostile (adj)	margin (n) **AW**
commence (v) **AW**	inclination (n) **AW**	notorious (adj)
diplomatic (adj)	join forces (v phr)	spy (n)
flourish (v)	legend (n)	ultimatum (n)

ACTIVITY 10 | Word associations

Circle the word or phrase that is most closely related to the word on the left.

1. ally	unfriendly	friendly
2. commence	finish	start
3. flourish	do well	have difficulties
4. fragile	fresh	weak
5. hostile	impossible	unfriendly
6. legitimate	lawful	invalid
7. margin	edge	center
8. notorious	positive	negative
9. spy	secret	brief
10. ultimatum	first	last

ACTIVITY 11 | Collocations

Fill in the blank with the word that most naturally completes the phrase.

alliance	commence	hostile	margin	flourish

1. all classes _____ at 8 a.m.

2. include a one-inch _____

3. build a strong _____

4. _____ in a new environment

5. a(n) _____ environment

| diplomatic | fragile | legitimate | notorious | ultimatum |

6. an entirely _____ business

7. _____ for being late

8. deliver a(n) _____

9. an extremely _____ package

10. _____ relations

ACTIVITY 12 | Word forms

Complete each sentence with the correct word form. Use the correct form of the verbs.

NOUN	VERB	ADJECTIVE	ADVERB	SENTENCES
alliance ally	ally	allied		1. The two companies formed a strategic _____ to increase profits. 2. During World War II, the United States and the United Kingdom were _____.
diplomat diplomacy		diplomatic	diplomatically	3. Because of the trade war, _____ relations between the two countries are very strained. 4. Many countries believe that _____ should be tried before going to war.
	flourish	flourishing		5. With a bit more care and attention, the plants in your garden will _____. 6. The students are _____ because of their new textbooks.
legitimacy	legitimatize	legitimate	legitimately	7. Increasing health care costs is a _____ concern. 8. Students are _____ concerned about the costs of college tuition.
notoriety		notorious	notoriously	9. Al Capone was a _____ gangster in Chicago in the 1920s. 10. This intersection is _____ dangerous—there have been many car accidents here.

The Terracotta Army is a collection of terracotta sculptures depicting the armies of Qin Shi Huang, the first emperor of China.

ACTIVITY 13 | Vocabulary in writing

Choose five words from Words to Know. Write a complete sentence with each word.

1. _____

2. _____

3. _____

4. _____

5. _____

WRITING

ACTIVITY 14 | Writing a research paper

Follow the steps to write a research paper.

Step 1: Understand the assignment

Research Paper Assignment

Length: 1,000 words

Choose one of the topics below or a topic assigned by your teacher:

- An exploration of the purpose of China's Terracotta Army

- How to improve the efficiency of renewable energy sources

- The development and use of the International Space Station

- One or more ways coffee has influenced the world

- An analysis of the rise and fall of print media

Your paper must include:

- an interesting title
- an introduction that describes the topic of your paper and has a clear thesis statement
- body paragraphs that include quotations, paraphrases, and other supporting information from your research
- a minimum of three sources including at least two sources from an academic journal
- a conclusion that restates your thesis statement
- clear headers
- in-text citations
- a reference section at the end of the paper

Now answer the following questions.

1. Can you select your own topic? _____ Is there a specific topic? _____ If so, are you allowed to modify the topic? _____

2. How long is the research paper expected to be? _____

3. How many outside sources are required? _____ What types of sources are required? _____

4. What type of citation is expected? APA? MLA? Other? _____

Step 2: Choose a topic

Based on the instructions in the Research Paper Assignment, decide which topic you are going to research. Write your topic.

_____

Step 3: Brainstorm questions about the topic

Write five questions you would like to research for your topic.

Possible questions:

_____

_____

_____

_____

_____

Step 4: Find sources

Use a search engine like Google Scholar to find five credible sources for your paper.

	TITLE	SOURCE	AUTHOR	YEAR	PAGE REFERENCE
1.					
2.					
3.					
4.					
5.					

Step 5: Read and take notes

Write quotations or other pieces of evidence from each source that might prove helpful in your research paper.

1. _____

2. _____

3. _____

4. _____

5. _____

Step 6: Write a thesis statement

In developing your thesis, consider such questions as "What is my topic?" and "What is my position on this topic?" Think about the reasoning behind your position on the topic, and develop a thesis statement from these ideas. Write it here.

_____

_____

Step 7: Outline

On a separate piece of paper, write an outline to help you create a more detailed plan for your essay. Use your ideas from the previous steps. Then exchange your outline with a partner. Use the Peer Editing Form 1 for Outlines in the *Writer's Handbook* to help you comment on your partner's work.

Step 8: Locate specific information for the outline

Use your partner's feedback to revise your outline. What are three areas of your outline for which you need to locate more information or more sources?

Step 9: Organize your notes

Decide which notes are important for which parts of your outline. Use a highlighting system to organize your notes.

Step 10: Write the first draft

Use your outline and the feedback received to write the first draft of your research paper.

Step 11: Get feedback

Exchange your first draft with a partner. Then use Peer Editing Form 8 in the *Writer's Handbook* to help you to comment on your partner's writing.

Step 12: Write the final draft

Use the feedback to identify where you could improve your paper. Then write as many drafts as necessary to produce a good paper. Remember to proofread your research paper before you submit it to find any errors.

Additional Topics for Writing

Topics for research papers are often highly specialized. In considering the suggested topics below, think about why they would be effective topics for research papers and how they can help you to generate your own ideas about an effective subject for research and writing.

TOPIC 1: The Trail of Tears and its effects on U.S. history

TOPIC 2: People's right to privacy—and to be forgotten—in the digital age

TOPIC 3: Effective strategies for discouraging tax evasion

TOPIC 4: The ethical implications of cloning

WRITER'S HANDBOOK

UNDERSTANDING THE WRITING PROCESS

As you learned in Unit 2, writing is a process. Writers rarely write an essay from introduction to conclusion in one sitting. Instead, they follow certain steps. Use these steps as a guideline when you write, keeping in mind that you can return to any step at any time as you develop your essays.

Step 1:   Choose a Topic

Step 2:   Brainstorm

Step 3:   Outline

Step 4:   Write the First Draft

Step 5:   Get Feedback from a Peer

Step 6:   Reread, Rethink, Rewrite

Step 7:   Proofread the Final Draft

Steps in the Writing Process

Step 1: Choose a Topic

Sometimes you will be asked to write an essay on a broad topic such as "an influential person." In this case, you can choose any person as long as you can clearly show how that person has influenced you or others. In addition, you should try to choose a topic that you are interested in.

For this example, imagine that the topic was given: "Write an essay in which you discuss one aspect of being a vegetarian." As you consider the assignment, think about what kind of essay you want to write:

- A comparison of two types of vegetarian diets
- A historical account of vegetarianism
- An argument that being a vegetarian is better than being an omnivore

The type of essay you write (argument, comparison, etc.) will depend on the topic you choose (or are given) and the ideas you decide to develop.

Step 2: Brainstorm

Write every idea about your topic that comes to mind. Some of these ideas will be better than others; write them all. The main purpose of brainstorming is to write as many ideas as possible. If one idea looks promising, circle it or put a check next to it. If you write an idea that you know right away you are not going to use, cross it out.

Brainstorming methods include making lists, clustering similar ideas, or diagramming. Here is an example of one student's brainstorming diagram on the topic "being a vegetarian."

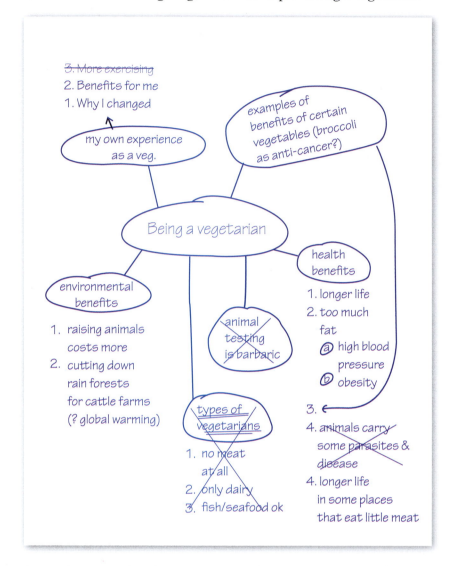

As you can see, the student considered many aspects of being a vegetarian. As she organized her ideas, she wrote "examples of benefits of certain vegetables" as one piece of supporting information. Then she realized that this point would be good in the list of health benefits, so she drew an arrow to show that she should move it there. Since one of her brainstorming ideas (types of vegetarians) lacked supporting details and was not related to her other notes, she crossed it out.

How can you get information for this brainstorming exercise?
- You might search online for an article about vegetarianism.
- You could write a short questionnaire to give to classmates asking them about their personal knowledge of vegetarian practices.
- You could interview an expert on the topic, such as a nutritionist.

Note that any information you get from an outside source needs to be credited in your essay. As you get information, keep notes on your sources. See "Citing Sources" later in this *Writer's Handbook* for more information on citing outside sources and referencing.

Step 3: Outline

Next, you should write an outline for your essay. Here is a possible outline based on the brainstorming notes.

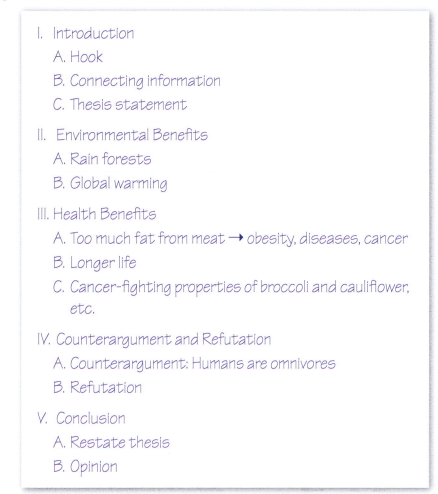

I. Introduction
  A. Hook
  B. Connecting information
  C. Thesis statement

II. Environmental Benefits
  A. Rain forests
  B. Global warming

III. Health Benefits
  A. Too much fat from meat → obesity, diseases, cancer
  B. Longer life
  C. Cancer-fighting properties of broccoli and cauliflower, etc.

IV. Counterargument and Refutation
  A. Counterargument: Humans are omnivores
  B. Refutation

V. Conclusion
  A. Restate thesis
  B. Opinion

Supporting Details

After you have chosen the main points for your essay, you need to develop some supporting details. You should include examples, reasons, explanations, definitions, or personal experiences.

One common technique for generating supporting details is to ask information questions about the topic: *Who? What? When? Where? Why? How?*

SUPPORT

What benefits does eating vegetables have?

How much longer do vegetarians live?

Why is eating meat a problem?

Step 4: Write the First Draft

In this step, you use information from your brainstorming and outline to draft the essay.

When you write your first draft, pay attention to the language you use. Use a variety of sentence types. Consider your choice of vocabulary, and include specific terminology when possible. Avoid using informal or conversational language.

This first draft may contain errors, such as misspellings, incomplete ideas, and punctuation errors. At this point, you should not worry about correcting the errors. The focus should be on putting your ideas into sentences.

As you write the first draft, you may want to add or remove information. In some cases, your first draft may not follow your outline exactly. That is OK. Writers do not always stick with their original plan or follow the steps in the writing process in order. Sometimes they go back and forth between steps. The writing process is much more like a cycle than a line.

Step 5: Get Feedback from a Peer

Peer editing is important in the writing process. You do not always see your own mistakes or places where information is missing because you are too close to your own writing. Ask someone to read your draft and give you feedback. Choose someone that you trust and feel comfortable with. While some people feel uneasy about peer editing, the result is almost always a better essay. You can use the Peer Editing Forms in this *Writer's Handbook* as tools to help your peer editors. Your teacher may also give you feedback on your first draft. As you revise, consider all comments carefully.

Step 6: Reread, Rethink, Rewrite

This step consists of three parts:
1. Reread your essay and any comments from your peers or teacher.
2. Rethink your writing and address the comments.
3. Rewrite the essay.

Step 7: Proofread the Final Draft

Proofreading is the final step. It means reading for grammar, punctuation, and spelling errors and seeing if the sentences flow smoothly. One good way to proofread your paper is to set it aside for several hours (or a day or two). The next time you read it, your head will be clearer, and you will be more likely to see any problems.

On the next two pages is a first draft of the essay on being a vegetarian. It includes comments from the teacher.

Reasons to Be a Vegetarian

1   Do you like burgers? Eating meat, especially beef, is an interesting part of daily life around the world. *wrong transition?* In addition, this *word choice* high eating of meat is a major contributing *word choice* thing that *word choice* makes many deaths, including deaths from heart-related problems. Vegetarianism has caught on slowly in some parts of the world. *transition?* ^Vegetarianism is a way of life that can help improve not only the quality of lives but also people's longevity.

Be sure your thesis matches your main points. Body par 1 seems to be about environmental impact. Also, you start with burgers but never mention them again. Check your word choice and use of parallel structure.

2   Because demand for meat is so high, cattle are being raised in areas where the rain forest once stood. [As rain forest land is cleared in order to make room for the cattle ranches]. *frag* The environmental balance is being upset. This could have serious consequences for us in both the near and long term. How much of the current global warming is due to man's disturbing the rain forest?

You need a topic sentence with your first supporting idea: the first reason to be a vegetarian. And add a concluding sentence that restates your main idea.

3   Meat contains a high amount of fat. Eating this fat has been connected in research with certain kinds of cancer. Furthermore, eating animal fat can lead to obesity, and obesity can cause different kinds of disease. *what does "this" refer to?* This results in high blood pressure. Meat is high in cholesterol, and this adds to the health problems. With the high consumption of animal fat, it is no wonder that heart disease is a leading killer.

Try a more specific topic sentence relating to health and your thesis.

4   On the other hand, eating a vegetarian diet can improve a person's

necessary?

health. And vegetables <u>taste</u> good. In fact, it can even save lives. Eating

certain kinds of vegetables such as broccoli, brussels sprouts, and cauliflower,

s/v agr

<u>have been</u> shown to reduce the chance of colon cancer. Vegetables do not

contain the "bad" fats that meat does. Vegetables do not contain cholesterol

either. People with vegetarian diets live longer lives.

Look for places to combine short sentences. Remember that you need a counterargument and a refutation in an argument essay. Add these after your main arguments and before your conclusion.

5   Although numerous studies have shown the benefits of vegetarianism

for people in general, I know how my life has improved since I decided to

give up meat. In 2010 I saw a show that discussed the problems connected

to animals raised for food. After I saw this show, I decided to try life without

meat. Although it was difficult at first, I have never regretted my decision.

I feel better than before and people tell me I look good. Being a vegetarian

has many benefits. Try it.

This is a good first draft. I can see that you thought about your topic as you give some interesting reasons for being a vegetarian. Work on your thesis, topic sentences, and conclusion. Add a counterargument and a refutation. Consider making a recommendation in your conclusion. As you rewrite, ask yourself this question: Why should a person become a vegetarian? Your essay is supposed to answer this question.

Now read the final essay this student turned in to her teacher.

Reasons to Be a Vegetarian

1   Eating meat, especially beef, is an integral part of many cultures. Studies show, however, that the consumption of large quantities of meat is a major contributing factor toward a great many deaths, including the unnecessarily high number of deaths from heart-related problems. Although it is not widely adopted in many countries, vegetarianism is a way of life that can have a positive impact on the environment and people's health.

2   Surprising as it may sound, vegetarianism can have beneficial effects on the environment. Because demand for meat animals is so high, cattle are being raised in areas where rain forests once stood. Rain forests have been cleared to make room for cattle ranches, upsetting the environmental balance. One important impact of this kind of deforestation is increased temperatures, which contribute to global warming. If people consumed less meat, the need to clear land for cattle would decrease, helping to restore the ecological balance.

3   More important at an individual level is the question of how eating meat affects a person's health. Meat, unlike vegetables, can contain large amounts of fat. Eating this fat has been connected—in some studies —to certain kinds of cancer. If people cut down on the amount of meat they ate, they would automatically be lowering their risk of disease. Furthermore, eating animal fat can lead to obesity, which can cause numerous health problems. For example, obesity can cause people to become physically inactive, forcing their hearts to have to work harder. This results in high blood pressure. Meat is also high in cholesterol, and this only adds to health problems. Eliminating meat from their diet and eating vegetarian food would help people reduce their risk of certain diseases.

4   If people followed vegetarian diets, they would not only be healthier, but also live longer. Eating certain kinds of vegetables, such as broccoli, brussels sprouts, and cauliflower, has been shown to reduce the chance of contracting colon cancer later in life. Vegetables do not contain the "bad" fats that meat does. Vegetables do not contain cholesterol, either. Furthermore, native inhabitants of areas of the world where people eat more vegetables than meat, notably certain areas of Central Asia, routinely live to be over one hundred years old.

5   Some people argue that, human nature being what it is, it is unhealthy for humans not to eat meat. These same individuals say that humans are naturally omnivores and cannot help wanting to consume a juicy piece of red meat. However, anthropologists have shown that early humans ate meat only when other foods were not abundant. Humans are inherently herbivores, not omnivores.

6   Numerous scientific studies have shown the benefits of vegetarianism for people in general. There is a common thread for those people who switch from eating meat to consuming only vegetable products. Although the change of diet is difficult at first, most people never regret their decision to become a vegetarian. As more and more people are becoming aware of the risks associated with meat consumption, they too will make the change.

PUNCTUATION

Commas

The comma has different functions. Here are some of the most common:

1. **A comma separates a list of three or more things.**
    She speaks French, English, and Chinese.
    He speaks French and English. (No comma is needed with two items.)

2. **A comma separates two sentences connected by a coordinating conjunction such as *and, but, or, so, for, nor,* and *yet*.**
    Six people took the course, but only five of them passed the test.
    Students can register for classes in person, or they can register by email.

3. **A comma is used to separate an introductory word or phrase from the rest of the sentence.**
    In conclusion, doctors are advising people to take more vitamins.
    Because of the heavy rains, many of the roads were flooded.

4. **A comma is used in complex sentences with adverb clauses when the adverb clause comes before the main clause.**
    Although George Washington did not have a formal education, he was a political leader, military general, and the first president of the United States.

5. **A comma is used to separate an appositive from the rest of the sentence. An appositive is a word or group of words that renames a noun.**

    subject (noun)   **appositive**

    Washington, the first president of the United States, was a clever military leader.

6. **A comma is sometimes used with nonrestrictive or unnecessary adjective clauses. We use a comma when the information in the clause is unnecessary or extra.**

    The History of Korea, which is on the teacher's desk, is the main book for this class.

    (The name of the book is given, so the information in the adjective clause is not necessary to help the reader identify the book.)

    The book that is on the teacher's desk is the main book for this class.

    (The information in the adjective clause is necessary to identify which book. In this case, do not set off the adjective clause with commas.)

Apostrophes

Apostrophes have two basic uses in English. They indicate either a contraction or a possession. Note that contractions are seldom used in academic writing.

Contractions: Use an apostrophe in a contraction in place of the letter or letters that have been deleted.

he's (he is *or* he has), they're (they are)
I've (I have), we'd (we would *or* we had)

Possession: Add an apostrophe and the letter *s* after the word. If a plural word already ends in *s*, then just add an apostrophe.

yesterday's paper
the boy's books
the boys' books

Quotation Marks

Here are three of the most common uses for quotation marks.

1. **To mark the exact words that were spoken by someone:**

The king said, "I refuse to give up my throne." (The period is inside the quotation marks.)
"None of the solutions is correct," said the professor. (The comma is inside the quotation marks.)

2. **To mark language that a writer has borrowed from another source:**

The dictionary defines gossip as a "trivial rumor of a personal nature," but I would add that it is usually malicious.
This research concludes that there was "no real reason to expect this computer software program to produce good results."

3. **To indicate when a word or phrase is being used in a special way:**

The king believed himself to be the leader of a democracy, so he allowed the prisoner to choose his method of dying. According to the king, allowing this kind of "democracy" showed that he was indeed a good ruler.

Semicolons

The function of a semicolon is similar to that of a period. However, a semicolon suggests a stronger relationship between the sentences.

Joey loves to play tennis. He has been playing since he was ten years old.

Joey loves to play tennis; he has been playing since he was ten years old.

Both sentence pairs are correct. Notice that *he* is not capitalized in the second example.

A semicolon is often used with transition words like *however, therefore,* and *in addition.*

The price of gas is increasing; therefore, more people are taking public transportation.

SENTENCE TYPES

English has three basic types of sentences: simple, compound, and complex. These labels indicate how the information in a sentence is organized, not how difficult the content is.

Simple Sentences

Simple sentences usually contain one subject and one verb.

        S   V
      Children <u>love</u> electronic devices.

       V   S   V
      <u>Does</u> **this** <u>sound</u> like a normal routine?

Sometimes simple sentences can contain more than one subject or verb.

       S   S   V
      Brazil and **the United States** <u>are</u> large countries.

       S   V   V
      <u>Brazil</u> **is** in South America and **has** a large population.

Compound Sentences

Compound sentences are usually made up of two independent clauses. The two clauses are connected with a coordinating conjunction such as *and, but, or, yet, so,* and *for.* A comma is used before the coordinating conjunction.

      Megan studied hard**, but** she did not pass the final test.

Complex Sentences

Complex sentences contain one independent clause and at least one dependent clause. In most complex sentences, the dependent clause is an adverb clause. (Other complex sentences have dependent adjective clauses or dependent noun clauses.) Adverb clauses begin with subordinating conjunctions, such as *while, although, because,* and *if.*

In the examples below, the adverb clauses are underlined, and the subordinating conjunctions are boldfaced. Notice that the subordinating conjunctions are part of the dependent clauses.

      independent clause   dependent clause

The hurricane struck **while** <u>we were at the mall</u>.

      dependent clause   independent clause

<u>**After** the president gave his speech</u>, he answered the reporters' questions.

Dependent clauses must be attached to an independent clause. If they are not attached to another sentence, they are called fragments or incomplete sentences. Look at these examples:

Fragment: After the president gave his speech.
Complete Sentence: After the president gave his speech, he answered the questions.

CONNECTORS

Using connectors will help your ideas flow. Three types of connectors are coordinating conjunctions, subordinating conjunctions, and transitions.

Coordinating Conjunctions

Coordinating conjunctions join two independent clauses to form a compound sentence. Use a comma before a coordinating conjunction in a compound sentence.

Independent clause, + coordinating + independent clause.
conjunction

The exam was extremely difficult, **but** all of the students received a passing score.

Subordinating Conjunctions

Subordinating conjunctions introduce a dependent clause in a complex sentence. When a dependent clause begins a sentence, use a comma to separate it from the independent clause.

Dependent clause, + independent clause.

Although the exam was extremely difficult, all of the students received a passing score.

Subordinating conjunction

When a dependent clause comes after an independent clause, no comma is used.

Independent clause + dependent clause.

All of the students received a passing score **although** the exam was extremely difficult.

subordinating conjunction

Transition Words

Transition words show the relationship between ideas in sentences. A transition followed by a comma can begin a sentence.

Independent clause. Transition, independent clause.

The exam was extremely difficult. **However,** all of the students received a passing score.

A transition word followed by a comma can also come after a semicolon. Notice that in the independent clause that follows the semicolon, the first word is not capitalized.

Independent clause. transition, independent clause.

The exam was extremely difficult; **however,** all of the students received a passing score.

Here is a chart summarizing kinds of connectors and their purpose.

PURPOSE	COORDINATING CONJUNCTIONS	SUBORDINATING CONJUNCTIONS	TRANSITIONS
To give an example			For example, To illustrate, Specifically, In particular,
To add information	and		In addition, Moreover, Furthermore,
To signal a comparison			Similarly, Likewise, In the same way,
To signal a contrast	but yet	while although	In contrast, However, On the other hand, Conversely, Instead,
To signal a refutation		although even though	On the contrary, Nevertheless, However, Even so,
To emphasize			In fact, Actually,
To clarify			In other words, In simpler words, More simply,
To give a reason/cause	for	because since	
To show a result	so		As a result, As a consequence, Consequently, Therefore, Thus,
To show time relationships		after as soon as before when while until since whenever as	Afterward, First, Second, Next, Then Finally, Subsequently, Meanwhile, In the meantime,
To signal a condition		if even if unless provided that when	
To signal a purpose		so that in order that	
To signal a choice	or		
To signal a conclusion			In conclusion, To summarize, As we have seen, In brief, To sum up,

USEFUL WORDS AND PHRASES

COMPARING	
In comparison,	Canada has provinces. **In comparison,** Brazil has states.
Compared to Similar to Like	**Compared to** these roses, those roses last a long time.
Both … and	**Both** models **and** real planes have similar controls.
Likewise, Similarily,	Students spend hours each day developing their language skills to enhance their writing. **Likewise,** ballerinas spend countless hours in the gym each week increasing their accuracy and endurance.

CONTRASTING	
In contrast,	Algeria is a very large country. **In contrast,** the U.A.E. is very small.
Contrasted with In contrast to	**In contrast to** Chicago, Miami has only two seasons: a very mild winter and a very long summer.
Although Even though Though	**Though** London in 1900 was quite different from London in 2000 in many ways, important similarities existed in population, technology, and transportation.
Unlike	**Unlike** Chicago, the problem in Miami is not the cold but rather the heat.
However,	Canada has provinces. **However,** Brazil has states.
On the one hand, On the other hand,	**On the one hand,** Maggie loved to travel. **On the other hand,** she hated to be away from her home.

SHOWING CAUSE AND EFFECT	
Because Since	**Because** their races are longer, distance runners need to be mentally strong.
cause lead to result in	An earthquake **can lead to** tidal waves and can cause massive destruction.
As a result of Because of	**Because of** the economic sanctions, the unemployment rate rose.
Therefore, As a result,	Markets fell. **Therefore,** millions of people lost their life savings.

STATING AN OPINION

I believe / think / feel / agree that	**I believe that** using electronic devices on a plane should be allowed.
In my opinion / view / experience,	**In my opinion,** talking on a cell phone in a movie theater is extremely rude.
For this reason,	**For this reason,** voters should not pass this law.
There are many benefits / advantages / disadvantages	**There are many benefits** to swimming every day.

ARGUING

It is important to remember	**It is important to remember** that school uniforms would be worn only during school hours.
According to a recent survey,	**According to a recent survey,** the biggest fear of most people is public speaking.
For these reasons,	**For these reasons,** public schools should require uniforms.
Without a doubt,	**Without a doubt,** students ought to learn a foreign language.

GIVING A COUNTERARGUMENT

Proponents / Opponents (may) say	**Opponents** of uniforms **say** that students who wear uniforms cannot express their individuality.
One could argue that …, but	**One could argue that** working for a small company is very exciting, **but** it can also be more stressful than a job in a large company.
Some people believe that	**Some people believe that** nuclear energy is the way of the future.
Although it is true that	**Although it is true that** taking online classes can be convenient, it is difficult for many students to stay on task.

CITING SOURCES

When writing an essay, you should use you own words for the most part. Sometimes, however, you may want to use ideas that you have read in a book, in an article, or on a website, or even heard in a speech. It can make the essay more interesting, more factual, or more relevant to the reader. For example, if you are writing about a recent election, you may want to use a quotation from a politician. In this case, you must indicate that the words are not your own, but that they come from someone else. Indicating that your words are not original is called **citing**. In academic writing, it is necessary to cite all sources of information that are not original.

If you do not—whether intentionally or unintentionally—give credit to the original author, you are **plagiarizing**, or stealing, someone else's words. This is academic theft, and most institutions take this very seriously. To avoid plagiarism, it is important to use quotes or a paraphrase which includes an in-text citation, and add a reference or bibliography at the end of your writing.

Using Quotes

Quotations are used when you want to keep the source's exact words. Here are some verbs that are often used to introduce quotes.

argue	describe	insist	predict	say
claim	find	point out	report	state

Here are three examples of quoting a sentence from a text in APA style.

Original: There is absolutely no empirical evidence—quantitative or qualitative —to support the familiar notion that monolingual dictionaries are better than bilingual dictionaries for understanding and learning L2.

Quote 1: According to Folse (2004), "There is absolutely no empirical evidence—quantitative or qualitative—to support the familiar notion that monolingual dictionaries are better than bilingual dictionaries for understanding and learning L2" (p. 120).

Quote 2: While instructors continue to push for monolingual dictionaries, "there is absolutely no empirical evidence—quantitative or qualitative—to support the familiar notion that monolingual dictionaries are better than bilingual dictionaries for understanding and learning L2" (Folse, 2004, p. 120).

Quote 3: As Folse (2004) points out, "There is absolutely no empirical evidence—quantitative or qualitative—to support the familiar notion that monolingual dictionaries are better than bilingual dictionaries for understanding and learning L2" (p. 120).

Note that brief in-text citations in the body of your work are appropriate for quotes like these. However, you must also list the complete source at the end of your work.

Folse K. (2004). *Vocabulary myths: applying second language research to classroom teaching*. Ann Arbor: University of Michigan Press.

Paraphrasing

Sometimes you may want to paraphrase or summarize outside information. In this case, the same rules still hold true. If the ideas are not yours, they must be cited.

Original: Every year, the town of Vinci, Italy, receives as many as 500,000 visitors—people coming in search of its most famous son, Leonardo.

Paraphrase: Although a small town, Vinci is visited by many tourists because it is the birthplace of Leonardo da Vinci (Herrick, 2016).

Original: This quiet, unimposing hill town is relatively unchanged from the time of Leonardo.

Paraphrase: Herrick (2016) explains that even after 500 years, the town of Vinci has remained pretty much the same.

Herrick, Troy. "*Vinci: A Visit to Leonardo's Home Town.*" Offbeat Travel, Updated January 5, 2016, www.offbeattravel.com/vinci-italy-davinci-home.html.

Formatting APA and MLA Citations

The chart below shows how to format APA and MLA citations for various sources.

APA

SOURCE	INFORMATION TO INCLUDE	EXAMPLES
Book	**Quotation/Paraphrase** Author(s), year, and page number. **References** Author Last Name, Author Initial(s). (Year of publication). *Title of work.* Location: Publisher.	**Quotation/Paraphrase** According to Beronä (2008), "…" (p. 147). **References** Beronä, D. (2008). *Wordless books: The original graphic novels.* New York: Abrams.
Academic Journal	**Quotation/Paraphrase** Author(s), year, and page number. **References** Author Last Name, Author Initial(s). (Year of publication). Title of article. *Journal Title, Volume*(Issue), pages.	**Quotation/Paraphrase** As Bhattarchajee and colleagues (2017) propose, "…" (p. 4564). **References** Bhattarchajee, D., Sau, S., Das, J., & Bhadra, A. (2017). Free-ranging dogs prefer petting over food in repeated interactions with unfamiliar humans. *Journal of Experimental Biology, 220*(224), 4564-4660.
Online Article	**Quotation/Paraphrase** Author(s) and year. **References** Author Last Name, Author Initial(s). (Year of publication). Title of article. *Title of Online Site, Volume* (Issue number). Retrieved from (URL).	**Quotation/Paraphrase** Patel, Best, and Rabinowitz (2018) demonstrate the following: "…" **References** Patel, S., Best, S., & Rabinowitz, R. (2018). Sherlock Holmes and the case of the vanishing examination. *The American Journal of Medicine. 131*(11). Retrieved from https://www.amjmed.com/article/S0002-9343(18)30502-3/fulltext.
Newspaper/ Magazine	**Quotation/Paraphrase** Author(s), year, and page number. **References** Author Last Name, Author Initial(s). (Year and date of publication). Title of article. *Title of Newspaper/Magazine*, pages.	**Quotation/Paraphrase** Smith (2008) documents the necessary steps for an emergency: "…" (p. 3). **References** Smith, S. (2008, December 13). "What to do in case of emergencies." *USA Today*, 2–3.

MLA

SOURCE	INFORMATION TO INCLUDE	EXAMPLES
Book	**Quotation/Paraphrase** Last name of author(s), page number. **Works Cited** Last Name of Author, First Name. *Title of Book*. Publisher, Year.	**Quotation/Paraphrase** According to Beronä, "…." (147). **Works Cited** Beronä, David. *Wordless Books: The Original Graphic Novels*. Abrams, 2008.
Academic Journal	**Quotation/Paraphrase** Last name of author(s), page number. **Works Cited** Last Name of Author, First Name. "Title of Article." *Title of Journal*, vol., volume number, year, pages.	**Quotation/Paraphrase** As Bhattarchajee and colleagues propose, "…" (4564). **Works Cited** Bhattarchajee, Debottam, et al. "Free-Ranging Dogs Prefer Petting over Food in Repeated Interactions with Unfamiliar Humans." *Journal of Experimental Biology*, vol. 220, no. 224, 2017, pp. 4564-4660.
Online Article	**Quotation/Paraphrase** Last name of author(s). **Works Cited** Last Name of Author, First Name. "Title of Web Page." Title of Website, Publisher, Date published, URL. Date of access.	**Quotation/Paraphrase** Patel, Best, and Rabinowitz demonstrate the following: "…" **Works Cited** Patel, Sutchin, et al. "Sherlock Holmes and the Case of the Vanishing Examination." The American Journal of Medicine, Nov. 2018. www.amjmed.com/article/S0002-9343(18)30502-3/fulltext. Accessed 27 Nov. 2018.
Newspaper/ Magazine	**Quotation/Paraphrase** Last name of author(s), page number. **Works Cited** Last Name of Author, First Name. "Title of Article." *Name of Newspaper*, Date, pages.	**Quotation/Paraphrase** Smith documents the necessary steps for an emergency: "…" (3). **Works Cited** Smith, Steven. "What to Do in Case of Emergencies." *USA Today*, 13 Dec. 2008, pp. 2–3.

TEST TAKING TIPS

Before Writing

- Before you begin writing, make sure that you understand the assignment. Underline key words in the writing prompt. Look back at the key words as you write to be sure you are answering the question correctly and staying on topic.
- Take at least five minutes to plan before you start writing. First, list all the ideas you have about the topic. Then think about which ideas have the best supporting examples or ideas. Use this information to choose your main idea(s). Circle the supporting information you want to include. Cross out other information.
- Organize your ideas before you write. Review the list you have created. Place a number next to each idea, from most important to least important. In this way, if you do not have enough time to complete your writing, you will be sure that the most relevant information will be included in your essay.

While Writing

For Paragraphs

- Be sure that your topic sentence has a logical controlling idea. Remember that your topic sentence guides your paragraph. If the topic sentence is not clear, the reader will have difficulty following your supporting ideas.
- It is important for your writing to look like a paragraph. Be sure to indent the first sentence. Write the rest of the sentences from margin to margin. Leave an appropriate amount of space after your periods. These small details make your paragraph easier to read and understand.

For Essays

- Be sure that your thesis statement responds to the prompt and expresses your main idea. The thesis may also include your points of development. Remember that if your thesis statement is not clear, the reader will have difficulty following the supporting ideas in the body paragraphs.
- Readers will pay special attention to the last paragraph of your essay, so take two or three minutes to check it before you submit it. Make sure your concluding paragraph restates information in the introduction paragraph and offers a suggestion, gives an opinion, asks a question, or makes a prediction.

For Either Paragraphs or Essays

- Do not write more than is requested. If the assignment asks for a 150-word response, be sure that your writing response comes close to that. Students do not get extra points for writing more than what is required.
- Once you pick a side (agree or disagree), include only the ideas that support that side. Sometimes you may have ideas for both sides. In this case, choose the side that is easier for you to write about. If you do not have an opinion, choose the side you can write about best, even if you do not believe in it. You receive points for your writing skills, not your personal beliefs.

Word Choice

- Avoid using words such as *always*, *never*, *all*, and *none*. You cannot give enough proof for these words. Instead, use words such as *probably*, *often*, *most*, *many*, *almost never*, and *almost none*.
- Avoid using general or vague vocabulary. Words such as *nice*, *good*, and *very* can often be changed to more specific terms, such as *friendly, fabulous,* and *incredibly*. Be more specific in your word choice.
- Avoid conversational or informal language in academic writing.

Development

- Avoid information that is too general. When possible, give specific examples. Good writers want to show that they have thought about the subject and provide interesting and specific information in their writing.

After Writing

- Leave time to proofread your paragraph or essay. Check for subject-verb agreement, correct use of commas and end punctuation, and for clear ideas that all relate to the topic sentence (paragraphs) or thesis statement (essay).
- Check for informal language such as contractions or slang. These do not belong in academic writing.

Managing Time

- It is common to run out of time at the end of a writing test. Once you have written your introduction and the body paragraphs, check your remaining time. Then read through what you have written to check for the clarity of your ideas. If you are running out of time, write a very brief conclusion.

PEER EDITING FORMS

Peer Editing Form 1 for Outlines

Reader: _____   Date: _____

1. What is the topic of the essay? _____

2. Is there an effective hook?   ☐ Yes   ☐ No

3. Is the thesis statement clear?   ☐ Yes   ☐ No

   If not, explain. _____

4. What do you expect to read about in this essay? _____

   _____

5. How many paragraphs are going to be in the essay? _____

6. Does the topic sentence in each body paragraph relate to the thesis?   ☐ Yes   ☐ No

   If not, explain. _____

7. What kind of ending will the essay have—a suggestion, prediction, question, or opinion?

   _____

8. Do you have any questions about the outline?   ☐ Yes   ☐ No

   If yes, write them here: _____

   _____

Peer Editing Form 2

Reader: _____ Date: _____

1. What is the title of the essay? _____

2. Does the introduction have an effective hook?   ☐ Yes   ☐ No

   If not, how can it be better? _____

   _____

3. Write the thesis statement here: _____

   _____

   What suggestions do you have for improving it? _____

   _____

4. Based on the introduction, what do you expect to read about in this essay? _____

   _____

5. Does each body paragraph have a topic sentence related to the thesis statement? ☐ Yes   ☐ No

   If not, explain: _____

6. Does the essay include at least two vocabulary words or phrases from the unit? If yes, list them here:

   _____

7. Which of the following does the writer do in the conclusion?

   ☐ restate the thesis statement   ☐ ask a question   ☐ make a prediction

   ☐ offer a suggestion   ☐ give an opinion

8. What do you like best about this essay? _____

   _____

9. Are there any places where you want more information?   ☐ Yes   ☐ No

   If yes, where? _____

Peer Editing Form 3

Reader: _____ Date: _____

1. What is the title of the essay? _____

2. Does the introduction have an effective hook? ☐ Yes ☐ No

   If not, how can it be better? _____

3. Write the thesis statement here: _____

   _____

   What suggestions do you have for improving it? _____

   _____

4. Does each body paragraph have a topic sentence related to the thesis statement? ☐ Yes ☐ No

   If not, explain: _____

5. Does the essay include at least two vocabulary words or phrases from the unit? If yes, list them here:

   _____

6. Which of the following does the writer use in the conclusion?

   ☐ restate the thesis statement   ☐ ask a question   ☐ make a prediction

   ☐ offer a suggestion   ☐ give an opinion

7. What do you like best about this essay? _____

   _____

8. Are there any places where you want more information? ☐ Yes ☐ No

   If yes, where? _____

   _____

9. How many citations does the writer use? _____

10 Do you think this number is too low or too high? Why?

   _____

Peer Editing Form 4

Reader: _____ Date: _____

1. What is the topic of the cause-effect essay? _____

2. Which method does it follow? ☐ Focus-on-causes ☐ Focus-on-effects

3. Does the introduction have an effective hook? ☐ Yes ☐ No

   If not, how can it be better? _____

   _____

4. Write the thesis statement here: _____

   _____

   What suggestions do you have for improving it? _____

   _____

5. Does each body paragraph have a topic sentence related to the thesis statement? ☐ Yes ☐ No

   If not, explain. _____

6. Which connectors did the writer use to show cause or effect? _____

   _____

7. Does the essay include at least two vocabulary words or phrases from the unit?

   If yes, list them here: _____

8. Which of the following does the writer use in the conclusion?

   ☐ restate the thesis statement   ☐ ask a question   ☐ make a prediction

   ☐ offer a suggestion   ☐ give an opinion

9. What do you like best about this essay? _____

   _____

10. How many citations does the writer use? _____ Do you think this number is too low

    or too high? Why? _____

Peer Editing Form 5

Reader: _____ Date: _____

1. What is the topic of the comparison essay? _____

2. Which method does it follow? ☐ Block   ☐ Point-by-point

3. Does the introduction have an effective hook? ☐ Yes ☐ No

   If not, how can it be better? _____

4. Write the thesis statement here: _____

   _____

   What suggestions do you have for improving it? _____

   _____

5. Does each body paragraph have a topic sentence related to the thesis statement? ☐ Yes ☐ No

   If not, explain. _____

6. Which connectors did the writer use to show comparison or contrast? _____

   _____

7. Does the essay include at least two vocabulary words or phrases from the unit? If yes, list them

   here: _____

8. Which of the following does the writer use in the conclusion?

   ☐ restate the thesis statement   ☐ ask a question   ☐ make a prediction

   ☐ offer a suggestion   ☐ give an opinion

9. Are there any places where you want more information? ☐ Yes ☐ No

   If yes, where? _____

10. How many citations does the writer use? _____ Do you think this number is too low

   or too high? Why? _____

Peer Editing Form 6

Reader: _____ Date: _____

1. What is the topic of the reaction essay? _____

2. What type of prompt did the writer select? _____

3. Does the introduction have an effective hook?   ☐ Yes   ☐ No

    If not, how can it be better? _____

4. Write the thesis statement here: _____

    _____

    Does the thesis summarize and describe the prompt?   ☐ Yes   ☐ No

    What suggestions do you have for improving it? _____

    _____

5. Does each body paragraph have a topic sentence that states a reaction?   ☐ Yes   ☐ No

    If not, explain: _____

6. Does each body paragraph have supporting language for the reaction in the
    paragraph?   ☐ Yes   ☐ No

    If not, explain: _____

7. Does the essay include at least two vocabulary words or phrases from the unit? If yes, list them

    here: _____

8. Which of the following does the writer use in the conclusion?

    ☐ restate the thesis statement   ☐ ask a question   ☐ make a prediction

    ☐ offer a suggestion   ☐ give an opinion

9. What do you like best about this essay? _____

10. Are there any places where you want more information?   ☐ Yes   ☐ No

    If yes, where? _____

    _____

Peer Editing Form 7

Reader: _____ Date: _____

1. What is the topic of the argument essay? _____

2. Does the introduction have an effective hook? ☐ Yes ☐ No

   If not, how can it be better? _____

3. Write the thesis statement here: _____

   _____

   What suggestions do you have for improving it? _____

4. Does each body paragraph have a topic sentence related to the thesis statement? ☐ Yes ☐ No

   _____

   If not, explain: _____

5. Does the essay include a counterargument and refutation? ☐ Yes ☐ No

6. Does the essay include modals to control the tone? ☐ Yes ☐ No

   If yes, list them here: _____

7. Does the essay include at least two vocabulary words or phrases from the unit? If yes, list them

   here: _____

8. Which of the following does the writer use in the conclusion?

   ☐ restate the thesis statement   ☐ ask a question   ☐ make a prediction

   ☐ offer a suggestion   ☐ give an opinion

9. What do you like best about this essay? _____

   _____

10. How many citations does the writer use? _____ Do you think this number is too low

    or too high? Why? _____

Peer Editing Form 8

Reader: _____   Date: _____

1. What is the topic of the research paper? _____

2. Does the introduction have an effective hook?   ☐ Yes   ☐ No

    If not, how can it be better? _____

3. Write the thesis statement here: _____

    _____

    Do you have any suggestions for improving it? _____

4. Does each body paragraph have a topic sentence related to the thesis statement? ☐ Yes ☐ No

    _____

    If not, explain: _____

5. How many sources did the writer use? _____

    Does this meet the requirements in the original assignment?   ☐ Yes   ☐ No

6. Is every source cited in the paper?   ☐ Yes   ☐ No

    Is every citation listed in the reference list?   ☐ Yes   ☐ No

7. Does the essay include at least two vocabulary words or phrases from the unit? If yes, list them

    here: _____

8. Which of the following does the writer use in the conclusion?

    ☐ restate the thesis statement   ☐ ask a question   ☐ make a prediction

    ☐ offer a suggestion   ☐ give an opinion

9. What do you like best about this paper? _____

    _____

10. Are there any places where you want more information?   ☐ Yes   ☐ No

    If yes, where? _____

    _____

VOCABULARY INDEX

Word	Page	CEFR† Level	Word	Page	CEFR† Level	Word	Page	CEFR† Level
prey*	13	C2	revolutionize*	154	OFF LIST	tedious	5	C1
prospective*	84	C1	seek	57	B2	tempting*	78	B2
prosper	102	C2	seemingly	84	C1	thereby*	37	C1
radically*	78	C1	shift*	37	B2	tough*	36	B2
rank	129	C1	simulate*	109	OFF LIST	tragic	37	B2
rational*	37	C1	span*	78	C2	trigger*	147	C1
readily*	124	B2	spy	179	B1	ultimatum	179	OFF LIST
reciprocal	84	OFF LIST	staggering	124	C1	unambiguously*	78	OFF LIST
reign*	78	C1	strategize	36	OFF LIST	up to	37	OFF LIST
reluctance*	102	OFF LIST	subsequent*	5	C1	vastly	5	OFF LIST
reputable	129	C1	subsidized*	147	OFF LIST	verify	5	C1
retain*	17	C2	superior	84	C1	virtually*	37	B2
retreat	78	C2	suspend*	154	B2	vital	102	B2
reveal*	57	B2	sustainable*	154	C1	vulnerable	13	C2
revelation*	124	C2	taken aback	124	OFF LIST	without a doubt	59	OFF LIST

Every unit in *Great Writing* highlights key academic vocabulary, indicated by AW . These words have been selected using the Academic Word List (Coxhead, 2000) and the New Academic Word List (Browne, C., Culligan, B., & Phillips, J., 2013).

*These words are on the AWL or NAWL.

†Vocabulary was also chosen based on levels of The Common European Framework of Reference for Languages (CEFR). CEFR is an international standard for describing language proficiency. *Great Writing 5* is appropriate for students at CEFR levels C1–C2.

The target vocabulary is at the CEFR levels as shown.

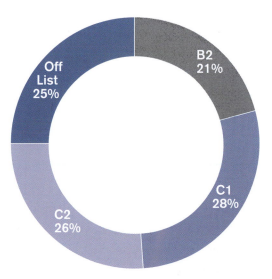

INDEX

A

Adverbs of degree with adjectives, 160–161
Analyzing a reaction essay, 126–128
Analyzing a research paper, 181–185
Analyzing organization of an argument essay, 151
Argument essays, 142–169
  analyzing organization of, 151
  body, 145
  brainstorming supporting ideas, 147, 168
  counterargument statements, 154–155
  defined, 144
  example, 148–151, 156–158
  first draft, 166
  introduction, 145
  organizing, 144
  outlining, 145, 151–152
  peer feedback, 167–168
  refutation statements, 154–155
  responding to teacher feedback, 166
  supporting details, 147
  thesis statements, 152
  topic selection, 146
  transitions, 154–156
  writing process, 168–169

B

Background information, 8
Block method, 74–75, 98–99
Body of essay, 4–5, 74–75, 81–82, 99, 124–125, 145
Body paragraph, 13
Brainstorming details, 125, 147
  focus-on-causes method, 74–75
  focus-on-effects method, 74
  organization, 77, 94
  supporting ideas, 147, 168
  topic questions, 174
  topics, 31–32, 46, 122, 125, 147
  with a Venn diagram, 101–102, 118
Building Better Sentences, 22–24, 44–45, 67–68, 90–93, 115–117, 135–138, 165–167, 188–190
Building Better Vocabulary, 20–22, 42–44, 64–66, 88–90, 113–115, 133–135, 162–164

C

Cause-effect essays, 72–95
  body, 74–75, 81–82
  brainstorming organization, 77, 94
  conclusion, 74–75, 82
  defined, 74
  first draft, 92
  focus-on-causes method, 74–75
  focus-on-effects method, 74
  introduction, 74–75, 81
  organization methods, 74–75
  outlining, 81–82

paraphrasing, 93
  responding to teacher feedback, 92
  studying example of, 78–81, 84–85
  supporting details, 76–77
  thesis statements, 82–83
  topic selection, 75–76
  transitions and connectors, 83–84
  writing process, 94–95
Citations, 4, 7
Citing sources, 180
Collocations, 20, 42, 65, 88, 113–114, 134, 162–163, 188–189
Combining sentences, 22, 45, 67–68, 91, 116, 165
Comparison essays, 96–119
  analyzing, 102–105
  block method, 98–99
  body, 99
  brainstorming details with a Venn diagram, 101–102, 118
  concluding paragraph, 99
  defined, 98
  organization methods, 98–99
  outlining, 106, 118
  peer editing, 118
  peer feedback, 118
  point-by-point method, 98–99
  thesis statements, 107
  topics, 100
  transitions and connectors, 109–111
  writing process, 117–118
Concluding paragraphs, 99, 125
Conclusion
  of essay, 4–5, 74–75, 82, 125
  of paragraph, 16–17
Connectors, 109–111
Consistent verb tense usage, 86
Controlling idea, 11
Counterargument statements, 154–155

E

Editing, 22, 35, 37, 44, 90, 115, 165, 168
Editing Form, 34–35
Essays
  argument, 5, 142–169
  citations, 4
  cause-effect, 72–95
  comparison, 96–119
  controlling idea, 11
  five-paragraph, 4
  introduction, 8
  narrowing topic, 30
  organization, 33
  parts of, 4–5,
  reaction, 120–141
  references, 4
  rhetorical modes, 5, 25
Evaluating sources, 175–176

F

Final drafts, 34, 38, 137, 166, 180
Finding sources, 176
First drafts, 46, 92, 180
Five-paragraph essays, 4
Focus-on-causes method, 74–75
Focus-on-effects method, 74

G

Grammar
  adverb clauses, 130–131
  adverbs of degree with adjectives, 160–161
  as…as; *not as…as*, 111
  consistent verb tense usage, 86
  modals, 158–159
  modifying nouns, 19
  noun and noun phrases, 19
  nouns modifying adjectives, 19
  parallel structure, 112
  passive voice, 185–186
  sentence fragments, 87
  subject-verb agreement, 40–41
  transitions and subordinating conjunctions, 131–133
  verb forms, 187
Great writing, elements of
  in an essay, 4–5
  in argument essays, 5, 144
  in cause-effect essays, 74
  in comparison essays, 98
  in five-paragraph essay, 4
  in reaction essays, 122
  in research papers, 172
  in the writing process, 28

H

Hook, 8–11

I

Identifying preferred prompts, 122–123
Introduction
  background information, 8
  hook, 8–11
  of essay, 4–5, 8, 74–75, 81, 99, 123, 145
  of paragraph, 8
  thesis statement, 8
  topic, 8

M

Modals, 158–159
Modifying nouns, 19
Noun and noun phrases, 19
Nouns modifying adjectives, 19

N

Narrowing a topic, 30
Noun and noun phrases, 19
Nouns modifying adjectives, 19

CREDITS

2-3 (spread) Jed Weingarten/National Geographic Image Collection; **6** Matt Moyer/National Geographic Image Collection; **9** Norbert Rosing/National Geographic Image Collection; **11** Hero Images/Getty Images; **14** Annick Vanderschelden photography/Moment Open/Getty Images; **15** George Grall/National Geographic Image Collection; **18** Clifton R.Adams/National Geographic Image Collection; **22** Joel Sartore, National Geographic Photo ARK/National Geographic Image Collection; **24** Catherine Karnow/National Geographic Image Collection; **26-27** (spread) Son Ha/Moment/Getty Images; **30** Gordon Wiltsie/National Geographic Image Collection; **36** Alf/Moment Unreleased/Getty Images; **38** shotbydave/E+/Getty Images; **40** Ralph Lee Hopkins/ National Geographic Image Collection; **41** © Aziz Abu Sarah; **43** Mark Conlin/Oxford Scientific/Getty Images; **47** Saro17/E+/Getty Images; **48-49** (spread) Jeremy Fahringer, Living Tongues Institute/Enduring Voices Project/ National Geographic Image Collection; **52** Incamerastock/Alamy Stock Photo; **53** Blaine Harrington III/Alamy Stock Photo; **60** mark phillips/Alamy Stock Photo; **62** (cr) Kheat/Alamy Stock Photo; (br) republica/ E+/Getty Images; **63** Aaron Rapoport/Corbis Historical/Getty Images; **66** Marco Grob/National Geographic Image Collection; **68** Joel Sartore/National Geographic Image Collection; **69** (cl) (cr) National Geographic Image Collection; **70** Tom Salyer/Alamy Stock Photo; **71** Frederic Courbet/Gallo Images/Getty Images; **72-73** (spread) © Hilary Swift; **75** Steven Kazlowski/Science Faction/Getty Images; **77** Jianan Yu/Reuters; **79** Chronicle/Alamy Stock Photo; **80** Boris SV/Moment/Getty Images; **90** Robert Harding picture library/ National Geographic Image Collection; **91** John Pratt/Keystone/Hulton Archive/Getty Images; **92** © Josh Brott; © Joel Sartore Photography; **96-97** (spread) Helena Wahlman/Maskot Images/Media Bakery; **99** David R. Frazier Photolibrary, Inc./Alamy Stock Photo; **101** (bl) Steve Raymer/National Geographic Image Collection; (br) Guntaphat Pokasasipun/Moment/Getty Images; **103** Caiaimage/Robert Daly/Getty Images; **107** (bl) Victor Fraile/Getty Images Sport/Getty Images; (br) Paul Zahil/National Geographic Image Collection; **110** Robert Muckley/Moment/Getty Images; **115** Design Pics Inc\National Geographic Image Collection; **119** © Annie Griffiths; **120-121** (spread) Albert Dros/National Geographic Image Collection; **123** Allik/Shutterstock.com; **124-125** (spread) National Geographic Image Collection; **127** © Mark Menjivar; **132** Matthew Williams-Ellis/ robertharding/Getty Images; **136** © Lucy G Design; **137** Rich Carey/Shutterstock.com; **138-139** (spread) National Geographic Image Collection; **141** Konstantin Tronin/Shutterstock.com; **142-143** (spread) Michael Nichols/National Geographic Image Collection; **145** Kike Calvo/National Geographic Image Collection; **148** thegoodphoto/iStock/Getty Images; **149** Michael Doolittle/Alamy Stock Photo; **153** Jodi Cobb/National Geographic Image Collection; **156** Rodrigo Friscione/Cultura/Getty Images; **159** Huw Jones/Lonely Planet Images/Getty Images; **161** Long Wei/Xinhua/Alamy Live News/Alamy Stock Photo; **164** Greg Vaughn/ Perspectives/Getty Images; **166** Bikeworldtravel/Shutterstock.com; **169** Sean Murphy/DigitalVision/Getty Images; **170-171** (spread) Tim Peake/ESA/Handout/Getty Images Publicity/Getty Images; **175** Sascha Kilmer/ Moment/Getty Images; **178** Fred Field/Portland Press Herald/Getty Images; **181** North Wind Picture Archives/ Alamy Stock Photo; **182** Bettmann/Getty Images; **187** Klaus Vedfelt/DigitalVision/Getty Images; **190** Zoonar GmbH/zhang zhiwei/Alamy Stock Photo.